The
TORRINGTON & MARLAND
Light Railway

Rod Garner

Kestrel Railway Books
PO Box 269
SOUTHAMPTON
SO30 4XR

www.kestrelrailwaybooks.co.uk

Printed by the Cromwell Press

ISBN 0954485971

Front cover:
"Peter" and "Mary" at the works.
An interesting scene at the works, probably prior to World War I, with a group of men having either just arrived for work, or about to leave for home. The train engine is "Peter", with "Mary" standing alongside. (The National Railway Museum)

DEDICATION

This book is dedicated to my wife **Anita,**
and to the memory of my late friend and sometime colleague,
Harold D Bowtell.

CONTENTS

Acknowledgements and Bibliography iv

Preface v

Chapter 1. The Development of Railways 1

Chapter 2. Devonshire in the 19th Century 15

Chapter 3. Rails to the Clay Works 27

Chapter 4. Locomotives and Rolling Stock 49

Chapter 5. Operation 65

Chapter 6. After the Narrow Gauge 81

Chapter 7. Conclusions 93

Appendix A. List of Guests 95

Appendix B. 3 Foot Gauge Steam Locomotives: 1879 – 1925 96

Appendix C. Bill of Quantities 97

Appendix D. Schedule of Prices 98

ACKNOWLEDGEMENTS

I had no idea when I started this exercise that I should cover so much ground or meet so many kind people in my researches. To check sources of already published material was a task in itself and to then go further, which was always to main object of the exercise, involved all kinds of areas previously unknown to me. Without the very kind assistance – willingly given – of a great many people, this work would not have got off the ground, let alone seen the light of day. I am sure that to list names is inviting the sin of omission but I do feel that many people should be mentioned, so if I have missed any names from this list, I apologise most sincerely and ask them to forgive the unintentional omission.

At this stage I must thank Mrs Marjorie Barraclough Fell, widow of Brian Barraclough Fell, the grandson of John Barraclough Fell, for making me welcome and allowing me access to family archives. Also to Alan Berryman who kindly took me through those archives. To Julian Fell and his family in the U.S.A., my thanks for a considerable amount of help and goodwill. My thanks are due to George Copp for arousing my interest in the first place and for great assistance along the way. John Hill of the Historical Model Railway Society was a tower of strength with early assistance in the form of contact names and material. The Beaford Archive has been of great help with photographs, as has John Pike of the Ball Clay Heritage Society. I am grateful to Matthew Cole for the drawings, in particular the one of the Torridge Viaduct.

Grateful thanks are due to Sue Scrutton the archivist of the Torrington Museum, the Torrington Library, the North Devon Record Office in Barnstaple, the Bideford & District Community Archive in Northam, Appledore Maritime Museum, the Public Record Office in Kew, and the British Library Newspaper archive in Colindale. Thanks also to Roger Kidner, Lord Clinton and the Clinton Estates – especially Mark Stevens, the Historical Model Railway Society – especially Allan Civil, Allan C. Baker, Barry Hughes, Keith Pearson, Douglas Stuckey, John Nicholas, and Ian Pringle. Also to the Institution of Civil Engineers, the Patent Office, the Narrow Gauge Railway Society, the Devonshire Association and the National Library of New Zealand.

BIBLIOGRAPHY

A great number of books, periodicals and other material have been consulted in the compilation of this work. The following list covers the most important of those consulted, but a complete list would be too extensive and even then possibly incomplete.

Lines to Torrington, John Nicholas
North Devon Clay, M.J. Messenger
Branch Lines to Torrington, Vic Mitchell and Keith Smith
John Barraclough Fell, Rev. A.N. Rigg
Mineral Railways, R.W. Kidner
A Regional History of the Railways of Great Britain: The West Country, David St John Thomas
A Regional History of the Railways of Great Britain: The Lake Counties, David Joy
The Oxford Companion to Railway History, edited by Jack Simmons and Gordon Biddle
The Patent Narrow Gauge Railways of John Barraclough Fell, E.A. Wade (N.G.R.S.)
Mr Fell Rides Again, E.A. Wade (*The Narrow Gauge* No. 149 – N.G.R.S.)
Minor Railways of England and their Locomotives, George Woodcock
Industrial Locomotives of South Western England, Industrial Railway Society
Devon, W.G. Hoskins
The North Devon & Cornwall Junction Light Railway, C.F.D. Whetmath and Douglas Stuckey
A Gazetteer of Railway Contractors & Engineers of the West Country, Lawrence Popplewell
Pentewan in the Past, R.E. Evans and G.W. Prettyman
The Pentewan Railway, M.J.T. Lewis
Devon's Waterways, A. Farquharson-Coe
Civil Engineering 1839-1889, Mike Chrimes
Transactions of the Devonshire Association, Various

PREFACE

I do not recall that I had ever heard of the Torrington & Marland Light Railway until just before my family and I came to live in Torrington. A lifelong interest in railways had made me aware that the railway once served Torrington, but that was it – or so I thought. It was not until later, when we had actually moved to the town, and a chance meeting delivered up some original and unpublished material relating to the construction of this little railway, that my interest was well and truly captured.

This is the story of a short, relatively unknown, narrow gauge railway built in a remote area of southwest England. It was built by the company it was to serve, for its own purposes and not, as was usual in those days, by a new company especially floated for the purpose and financed with public money. It lasted nearly forty five years and was then swept away by a standard gauge extension line, which finally bridged a gap in the railway system that had been under discussion in various formats for nearly one hundred years.

This little railway, from Great Torrington to the Marland Brick & Clay Company's works at Peters Marland, did not play a major part in the development of the railway network in Great Britain, nor did it have a lasting effect on local trade and industry. That is not to say that it was an insignificant and unimportant development in the story of railway building and the railway mania of the mid-nineteenth century. It was in fact an important stage in the development of the worldwide work of its engineer – John Barraclough Fell – and was a full-size practical demonstration of many of his patented ideas.

The line itself was known by a variety of names during its life; the engineer for the line used "Torrington & Marland Railway"; but "Claymoor Railway", "Marland Railway" and others were also used locally. After some consideration, I have used the name "Torrington & Marland Light Railway" as this appears both on the Ordnance Survey maps and also on the owners' letterhead paper.

The story of the Torrington & Marland is in many ways part of the story of Torrington and the surrounding area itself. We shall see how North Devon suffered from the delays in railway building in the area brought about by the after effects of the railway mania of the mid-1840s and of the "gauge wars" that were raging at the same time. This story is a classic case study of the effects of railway development on communities depending on whether, when, or how they were connected to the national network. Bringing the story up to date also forms an excellent study of the effects of the availability of public transport on rural communities at the turn of the millennium.

Much has been written about Devon, its railways, railway development generally and also about J. B. Fell. The clay works and the railways of the Torrington area have been written about before, but I felt there was more to know about this little line. I was keen to put the story into perspective, and to relate this little railway to the greater picture, and to take a look at the political, social and economic influences prevailing at the time both nationally and locally. Many personalities were involved in the creation and operation of this line; some directly, some indirectly; and I wished to explore each more fully wherever possible, with the aim of bringing a breath of real everyday life into the story.

Access to newly available archive material and to previously untapped sources has allowed me to pull together the strands of the various parts of the story, and I hope that my attempts to paint on a broad canvas whilst highlighting small detail will not be thought too ambitious. We shall consider such matters as the construction of the railway, and the design and construction methods used, as well as the influences that created them. The contractual aspects of the matter will also be considered, giving us an insight into business dealings of the day. I have sought to emphasise the local involvement at all stages, and research in this area has taken the most of the preparation time.

I have consulted many places, people, books, records and other archive sources in my researches and these are noted in the Bibliography or in the Acknowledgements section. I have been helped and guided by many people in producing this work and my thanks to them are expressed on the appropriate page of this book – without them I could not have produced much of what you are about to read. I hope that the results of my labours will be as fascinating to the reader as the unfolding story has been to me and if so, then I shall be very satisfied.

Rod Garner
Torrington
2005

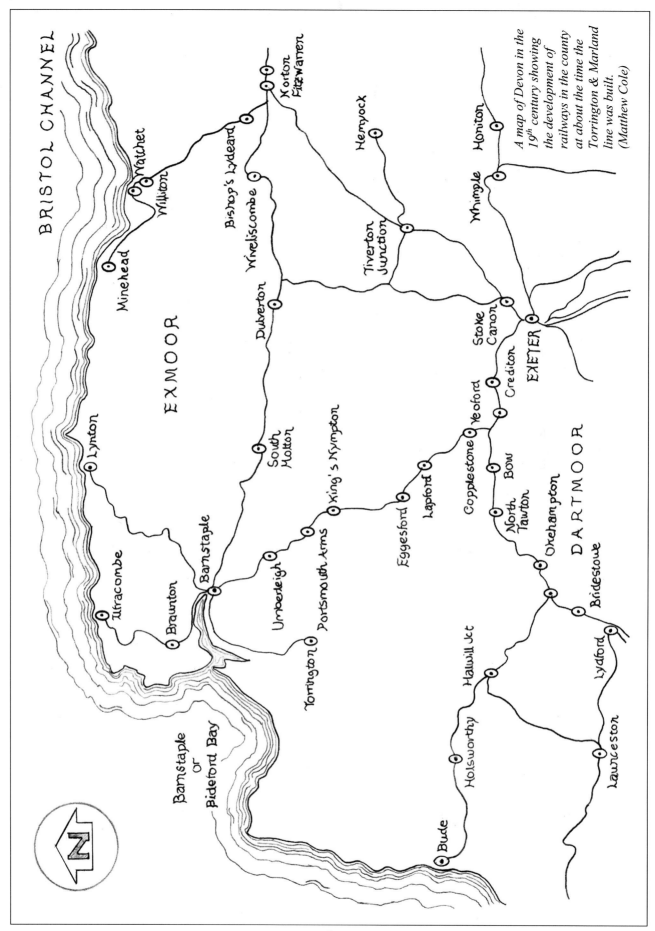

BRISTOL CHANNEL

Barnstaple or Bideford Bay

A map of Devon in the 19th century showing the development of railways in the county at about the time the Torrington & Marland line was built. (Matthew Cole)

EXMOOR

DARTMOOR

Ilfracombe
Lynton
Braunton
Barnstaple
Minehead
Watchet
Williton
Bishop's Lydeard
Wiveliscombe
Dulverton
South Molton
King's Nympton
Umberleigh
Portsmouth Arms
Torrington
Eggesford
Lapford
Copplestone
North Tawton
Bow
Okehampton
Bridestowe
Lydford
Launceston
Holsworthy
Halwill Jct
Bude
Norton Fitzwarren
Hemyock
Tiverton Junction
Whimple
Honiton
Stoke Canon
Crediton
Yeoford
Exeter

Chapter 1

THE DEVELOPMENT OF RAILWAYS

A General View

The first public railway to be opened for the conveyance of goods has generally been accepted as William Jessop's Surrey Iron Railway in July 1803, the Act for which was passed in 1801. Recent research indicates that, although this was probably the first Act for a public railway, one was passed the following year (1802) for the Carmarthenshire Railway, and the first section of this opened in May 1803. Whether any of the Surrey line was open by then is unclear, but the Company's dock at Wandsworth was opened in January 1802. Passengers were first catered for by the Oystermouth Railway, which opened in 1806. Richard Trevithick's famous Pen-y-darren locomotive first moved in 1804 and the first successful use of steam haulage was with the rack locomotive on the Middleton Railway in 1812. It is, however, the opening of the Stockton & Darlington Railway on 27th September 1825 that is often quoted as heralding the dawn of the steam railway age. Following the same simile, it may then be said that 15th September 1830 was the sunrise, for on that day the Liverpool & Manchester Railway was formally inaugurated as the world's first railway specifically built to carry both passengers and freight in trains hauled by steam locomotives. From this date the country was gripped by "railway fever" with Bills being presented for Parliamentary approval at such a rate as was impossible to control. Every merchant and inhabitant of almost every town wanted a railway, preferably on the main line, whether or not such a line was warranted by way of likely traffic, and surveyors seemed to appear round every corner plotting the best route for their particular proposed line. The public was, for the most part, seemingly keen to invest in almost any line that was proposed, and raising money was not a problem for most promoters. Parliament, having had some early attempts to control development largely ignored, threw in the towel and thereafter adopted a policy of *laissez-faire*, encouraging competition on the basis that free trade would be good for the public.

This first "Railway Mania" was halted by a general depression in trade between 1837 and 1842 but, once confidence had been regained and speculative money was again available, the pace of railway promotions surged ahead, culminating in the second "mania" of 1845–46. As an illustration of the growth of railway promotion, the mileage of new lines authorised between 1838 and 1843 was less than 250; in 1844 it had risen to 800 miles, at a cost of £20 million. The following year, this had risen to 2,816.25 miles – almost as many as in the period from 1821 to 1843, and two and a half times the total for 1836 – at £50 million. The following year (1846) saw 4,540.25 miles authorised, at a staggering £132 million. Even more staggering is that £132 million in 1846 is probably worth in the region of £7.3 billion at today's rates! In the three Parliamentary sessions of 1845 to 1848, some 650 Acts were passed for nearly 9,000 additional miles of railway. By now, things were really out of hand, with less than honest promoters taking money off the unsuspecting public (and the more knowledgeable as well) for the most unlikely and unfounded schemes. As we shall see later, many people felt that railways were a sound investment regardless as to whether they were likely to be viable or not. Of those lines sanctioned between 1845 and 1847, no less than 1,500 miles were abandoned within a couple of years.

This second wave of railway speculation was ended in a far more spectacular way when a world financial crash occurred, partly assisted by two bad harvests in 1846 and 1847. The English bank rate at the start of 1847 was 3% to 3.5%, but this had doubled to 7% by April and was at 10% by November, and in 1848 a world trade depression had hit. The failure of the Irish potato crop and the cheap import of foreign corn into Britain following the repeal of the Corn Laws added to the problems and many people, large and small, were bankrupted. Available money for investment in railway building dried up almost overnight. It must also be pointed out here that prior to the late 1850s, there was no such thing as limited liability. Shareholders in a company were liable without limit for its debts up to their share, and many small shareholders went to the wall in the collapse of the first "mania". It was not until the Joint Stock Companies Act and the Companies Act came into law in 1856 and 1862 respectively that limited liability restricted potential losses to the amount of a shareholder's investment. The railway business was rocked when financial manipulation of investment capital and share dividends by George Hudson was uncovered. Hudson controlled a huge railway empire – of the 5,000 plus miles open in 1848, Hudson controlled 1,450 – and had been proclaimed "The Railway King" in 1843 but his business practices were at best dubious, and some were, by modern standards, totally illegal. To attract investors, Hudson used new capital to pay dividends on other lines; in one instance paying 10% on a line before it had even opened! Such was the weight of Hudson's name that in 1844 he raised £2.5 million to build 3 branch lines without even giving details of where they were! Hudson's companies were self auditing but a protracted campaign by *The Times* against Hudson led to the appointment of Government auditors in 1849 as a result of which, Hudson, and some of his companies, were bankrupted. Public confidence in railway

Halwill & Beaworthy station.
0-6-0 Adams goods locomotive No 442 awaits the signal with an up goods train, circa 1907. The station later became Halwill Junction and, when the NDCJLR opened from Torrington in 1925, four lines converged on this lonely outpost.
(Tom Bartlett Postcard Collection, Berrynarbor, EX34 9SE)

speculation was lost – the bubble had burst and effectively brought to an end the period known as Railway Mania.

Prior to the coming of the railways, there was no such thing as standard time throughout the country. "Greenwich" time (or "London" time) was, of course, used in the capital and its surrounds, but elsewhere time varied considerably and consequently led to great confusion on the railways, especially those to the west. As long ago as 1808, the guards on the Irish Mail stagecoaches from Chester to Holyhead were required to carry a watch bearing Greenwich time and to advise the postmaster at each coaching inn of the "correct" time. The Liverpool & Manchester, the Great Western and the London & South Western Railways adopted Greenwich time from their inception, but the towns and cities they served often did not! Manchester Corporation adopted Greenwich time in 1847 and all clocks were reset. Resistance to a standard time was strong in the west of England and Wales, but the matter appears to have been settled on 2nd November 1852, when the Dean of Exeter ordered the cathedral clock to be advanced by fourteen minutes to align with Greenwich time! The railway companies began to install clocks on all

their stations, and public clocks became a common sight in towns and cities. Thus the railways had brought order to the business life of the nation in so far as time was concerned.

During this period of frenzied railway development, another factor was also inhibiting the growth of a unified railway network, and this was the question of gauge. George Stephenson had built the Stockton & Darlington and the Liverpool & Manchester to the "standard" gauge of four feet, eight and a half inches between the rails. It is said that he adopted this strange measurement as it was the gauge of the old colliery waggon-ways round Newcastle-on-Tyne. Most, but not all, of the railways up and down the country thereafter adopted this same gauge with one notable and important exception. In 1833 the directors of the Great Western Railway had appointed the young Isambard Kingdom Brunel as its engineer, and Brunel was not a man to be bound by custom or tradition when he was designing anything. Brunel was an engineer on the grand scale and with stability, safety and speed in mind he determined that the Great Western was to be built to a gauge of 7 feet and a quarter of an inch! And so it was! By June of 1838 the first section of the Great

Western's new main line from London Paddington was opened for traffic. Within a few years, the Great Western and it's associates had spread the broad gauge network to such an extent that many towns in Britain were served by both broad and standard gauge railways and trans-shipment of goods and passengers from one to another had become a nightmare. The matter became of such importance that on 9th July 1845, Parliament appointed a Commission to investigate the question of gauge and make recommendations. The Commission took evidence from both sides and from so-called independent experts, and even witnessed trials of each type of train. Early in 1846, the Commission reported to Parliament that two gauges were unacceptable and that whilst Brunel's broad gauge was in many ways superior to the standard gauge of Stephenson, the latter was so much more extensive that it was to be preferred. However, the Commission's report and recommendations were so fudged that mixed gauge lines – that is lines with three rails so as to allow for both broad and standard gauge trains on the same line – continued to be built, and the 7 foot was to remain in use by the Great Western for the next 54 years. The change of gauge was to plague railway operation until the last 7-foot gauge train ran on the Great Western from Paddington to Penzance on 20th May 1892.

The gauge question was not just a straight argument about which was the safer, faster and more economic; the actual need for a new line was subordinate to inter-company rivalry. The southwest of England, and in particular north and mid Devon, suffered greatly from the effects of the gauge war. The two great railway company competitors in this area were the Great Western Railway (the broad gauge champions) and the London & South Western Railway (standard gauge operators) and thus competition was very much gauge based, with each company trying to outdo the other in terms of laying its own gauge in each others territory. The battles for competing lines of different gauges lead to slow progress in actually building railways and thus, not only was railway development slow to start here, but building had hardly started when the end of Railway Mania came and capital dried up. The net effect of these two factors, lack of available capital for investment and the gauge war, was to effectively bring railway development in the area to a standstill for many years, to the continuing detriment of the area, as will be seen later.

Rails to North Devon

While it is true to say that large numbers of the population supported, even fought for, many of the railways proposed during the heady days of the Mania, there were also those who strenuously and actively opposed such proposals for one reason or another. Often they were the landowners over whose land the promoters wished to build the line, and who were convinced that this would be the ruination of their estates and livelihood. (There was also the school of thought that was convinced that the human body could not withstand the forces of travelling at twenty or thirty miles per hour, and that therefore all passengers would perish.)

In north and mid Devon however, the groundswell of public opinion was that railways were the future, and as early as 1831 the good folk of the area were convinced of the need for a railway to link the major port of Bideford in the north with the central and southern parts of the county. Bideford had been at the time of Elizabeth I the country's third largest port and was still, at this time, a major port. It was perceived that a railway would encourage the development of manufacturing in the county and facilitate the movement of goods from Bristol and South Wales. These were still largely shipped round Lands End to south Devon ports, greatly adding to the cost and causing long delays. Devon roads were still quite primitive and not capable of carrying much weight of traffic.

Capital was raised locally and a prominent local engineer, Roger Hopkins, was commissioned to survey and report on the feasibility of a railway line from Bideford to Okehampton. Hopkins was very active in the West Country with both roads and railways, and had been involved a couple of years earlier with the Dartmoor & Plymouth Railway, originally a horse-worked line but later converted to steam power. It served the isolated community at Princetown, high up on Dartmoor – the home of Dartmoor Prison. He was later to be main contractor on the Bodmin & Wadebridge Railway in 1834, and the engineer to the Llanidloes & Newtown Railway in 1852. He also built the first section of the Barnstaple Turnpike Road up the Sticklepath Hill out of Barnstaple.

Hopkins evidently undertook extensive surveys and detailed research work for this commission and reported at length towards the end of 1831. His report includes such matters as:

- Parochial reports on each parish to be traversed
- Anticipated revenue income with detailed listing of commodities to be carried with charges for each
- Current prices of various commodities at various towns and villages
- A listing of the various landowners involved showing length of their property to be traversed
- Distance and gradient figures throughout the proposed line.

Clearly Hopkins had done his work most thoroughly and presented a sound case, well supported by facts. When many large towns in the country were desperately trying to keep the railways at bay, feeling in Devon was quite different. Meetings supporting the proposals were held throughout the region, notably at Launceston, Tavistock, Plymouth, Okehampton and Bideford. To quote Hoskins "Even in the backwoods village of Winkleigh, a large and enthusiastic meeting was held in support of the proposed railway." It would be nice to think that the inhabitants of Winkleigh took this as a backhanded compliment!

Hopkins' basic proposal was for a new railway to run from the head of Lord Rolle's canal at Torrington to Meldon

Quarry near Okehampton, a total distance of just over 21 miles. The average gradient was to be 1 in 206 with a maximum of 1 in 98 for a short distance. Sidings were to be laid at the canal end of the line and 5 passing places of 70 yards in length were to be provided. The middle of these was for the two proposed steam locomotives to pass their trains. The other passing places were to be used as sidings for the delivery and collection of goods to the local areas. The gauge of the line was to be four feet eight inches, the extra half inch had clearly not yet gained universal acceptance.

Hopkins estimated the costs of building the line at £1,500 per mile, totalling £31,796 11s 0d with an overall total including land purchase, bridge building, surveys, and legal expenses of £47,251 11s 0d. This included £1,200 for "Two locomotive steam engines for propelling the Waggons on the Railway" and £900 for "Sixty Railways Waggons at 15 pounds each". A saving of £4,175 17s 0d would be made if the railway terminated at Okehampton rather than carrying on to Meldon Quarry. Hopkins' report, which is dated 24th October 1831, continues with estimates of annual operating costs of £1,480, traffic receipts of £5,713 (which included passenger receipts based upon a mere 15 journeys at 2/- each per day) giving a net income of £4,232. A two year construction period was envisaged.

A further report from Hopkins dated 8th November 1831 describes three alternative routes for the railway. The first assumes conversion of Lord Rolle's canal to a railway as part of the route with entry to Bideford on the west bank of the Torridge. The second assumes the canal remains in use and that the river is crossed and the line thus enters the port on the east bank. An interesting feature of this plan is the use of a "cut and cover" tunnel at Wear Giffard. To quote the report: "A deep cutting will be required in the meadow above the Church, of about three hundred yards in length, and this I propose to arch over the Railway and cover with turf, to prevent injury to the land." The third option was much as the first one, using the canal bed, but with a crossing of the Torridge at Landcross Point thus again entering Bideford on the east bank of the river. The mileages and costs given for the three alternatives are shown in Table 1.

Table 1. Options considered for proposed line to Torrington in 1831		
Option	**Mileage[1]**	**Cost**
1	8m 7f 6ch 30lks	£21,767 16s 8d[2]
2	8m 5f 9ch 63lks	£26,311 12s 0d
3	8m 7f 6ch 30lks	£19,093 6s 4d
1. Miles, furlongs, chains and links. 2. This figure was later amended to £21712.0.0d. in respect of a change to the design of bridge over the Torridge		

Hopkins also reported on a further proposal to link the railway to the town of Torrington itself. His main plans left the railway some two hundred feet vertically from the town, and about one mile by road from the town centre. The proposal was for an inclined plane some 550 yards in length from Torrington Bridge to Castle Hill. Access from the "main line" would be by 30 yards of level line at the bottom and a further 50 yards of level line would be provided at the top for loading/unloading. The plane would be laid with three rails, a passing place half way would enable up and down traffic to use the facility at the same time. Power to operate the chain driven lifting and lowering machinery would be provided by a water wheel fed by a two foot wide culvert from Torrington Mill, along the bed of the present canal and under the railway. Total cost was estimated at £1,700.

In spite of the detailed work and sound reasoning which had gone into these proposals, and the obvious determination locally for a railway, no initiative appears to have been taken to put the plans into action. Within a few years, supporters of the scheme appear to have deserted Hopkins' proposals to follow plans for a line to Exeter being put forward by the London & South Western Railway camp.

Meanwhile, in 1832, the year after Hopkins had reported to the worthies of Devon, Parliament authorised a broad gauge line from Exeter to Crediton in mid-Devon, but nothing was done and the powers lapsed. Thirteen years were to pass before the Exeter & Crediton Railway was again authorised by Parliament and by 22nd December 1846 the line was ready to open. The Bristol & Exeter Railway (broad gauge bedfellows of the GWR) were asked to operate the line, but a meeting of shareholders, heavily infiltrated by LSWR officials and supporters who had bought up shares, rejected the proposals out of hand. A new Board of Directors was appointed and the whole line was relaid to standard gauge. On 15th February 1848, the new line was ready to open but the Parliamentary Gauge Commissioners objected to the change of gauge as being outside the terms of the authorising Act. The opening was abandoned and the line left to rust! It was eventually reconverted to "broad" gauge and reopened on 12th May 1851 worked by the B&E but with the LSWR as majority shareholder. And so, 20 years after the Hopkins report, the railway had still only reached as far north as Crediton.

At about this time three other schemes were proposed for the area, all of which failed either through lack of capital or through failing to meet Parliamentary requirements. On 8th May 1846, the Bideford & Tavistock Railway was incorporated. The line was to be connected to the proposed extension of the South Devon Railway, which had recently been authorised. The engineers for the Company were none other than Messrs Rice and Thomas Hopkins, the sons of Roger Hopkins. (Rice Hopkins was to continue the family connection with railways and was one of the engineers building the West Somerset Mineral Railway in 1859/65.) The proposal was for a line from Tavistock to Okehampton

Torrington station in LSWR days.
Looking down to the station from the road leading up to the town. A train of LSWR four-wheelers is in the platform. The Torrington & Marland line has not yet been built, so the picture must have been taken between 1872 when the Torrington Extension Railway was opened from Bideford, and 1880. Note the fir trees, which were eventually felled when the road was realigned.
(The Beaford Archive)

where it would split; one route on to Hatherleigh, Torrington and Bideford; the other to Bow and Crediton where it would link with the Exeter & Crediton. A branch was also proposed to run to Barnstaple. The proposals came to nothing however as the South Devon decided against pushing up to Tavistock, although they eventually changed their minds! Just over a month later, on 6th June, the broad gauge North Devon Railway was incorporated. This was to start from an end-on junction with the Bristol & Exeter's branch at Tiverton and run through South Molton and Barnstaple to Bideford with a branch to Ilfracombe. Finally that same year the Cornwall & Devon Central Railway came into being with proposals to run from Exeter to Falmouth by way of Okehampton, Launceston, Bodmin and Truro. Support for this latter line was forthcoming from the LSWR but, like the other two, this also came to naught, as indeed did several other proposed routes between Plymouth and Tavistock.

In the meantime however, the Taw Vale Railway &

Dock Company had been authorised by Act of Parliament on 11th June 1838 as a "standard" gauge line from Fremington Pill to Barnstaple Bridge, with an extension to Fremington Quays authorised on 21st July 1845. The line opened in 1848, but used horses for haulage in its early days. On 7th August 1846 the Taw Vale Extension Railway & Dock Company was authorised to build a "broad" gauge line from Barnstaple to Exeter with branches to Bideford, South Molton and Ilfracombe. Once again the LSWR were involved in highly dubious share purchases to try and influence a change of gauge to protect it's own interests. In 1851 the Company was renamed the North Devon Railway and work started on construction in February 1852. Fremington and Barnstaple were finally connected to Exeter via Crediton on 1st August 1854 with broad gauge lines operated by the B&E for the first year. The contractor who built the line was Thomas Brassey, and the line was then leased to, and worked by, Brassey for some years. It is interesting at this stage to note that labourers' rates of pay at the start of construction of the North Devon line were 2/- per day, but that towards the end of the project these had risen to 2/6 and 3/- per day. Brassey was a great believer in paying good wages for good work, and here he found that higher rates of pay produced better and faster work, thus actually reducing the overall cost.

As early as 1845 plans had been made for an extension of the then proposed line from Fremington Pill to Barnstaple bridge to take it as far as Torrington but these had not come to fruition. The chairman of the Board of the Bideford Extension Company coincidentally was George Braginton. He was also then the lessee of the Rolle Canal and would clearly benefit from the extension to Bideford. March 1854 saw a public meeting in Torrington held for the purpose of advocating the extension from Bideford, but again nothing positive transpired. On 2nd November of the following year, the Bideford Extension Railway opened from Barnstaple to Bideford, again as broad gauge and again with Brassey as lessee and operator. W.R. Neale is again accepted as being the Engineer, although Joseph Locke may have had a hand in the matter. During 1862 and 1863, Brassey relinquished the lease, and control of the North Devon and Bideford extension lines was taken over by the LSWR and standard gauge track laid, thus becoming mixed gauge.

The position in 1863 was thus that the GWR and B&E had been running from Paddington to Exeter since 1844 on the broad gauge and the LSWR had opened their line from Waterloo to Exeter in 1860 as standard gauge. Barnstaple and Bideford were thus served by both gauges, and from 1st November 1874 the GWR line from Taunton to Barnstaple fully opened, thus increasing the scope of rail links to the area. However, there was increasing local pressure for the Bideford line to be extended to Torrington and beyond to provide a better link from the south and to open up that area still not served by the railway.

Clearly conscious of the public needs and demand, the Great Torrington Turnpike Trust had met in 1852 to consider how they could respond and, on 19th April, proposals were put forward for a direct coach service from Torrington to connect with the new North Devon line at Portsmouth Arms Station, thus providing an easier link to Exeter. A new section of the road would be built for the last part of the route. This would have avoided the long northward detour via Bideford and Barnstaple. However, at a meeting on 2nd April 1854 it was explained that the people of Torrington would have to pay for the new section of road and it appears that this was not an offer that Torrington felt like accepting! On 30th October 1854, the locally based coach firm of Pridham & Lake commenced a new service to Eggesford Station on the North Devon line (two stations further down from Portsmouth Arms) running from Wills Hotel in Torrington. A light coach "The Torrington" was provided for the service. The outward journey left Torrington at 8.00am and reached Eggesford in time for the 10.40am up train to Exeter. The return coach left at 4.42pm and arrived in Torrington at 7.00pm. William Pridham of Pridham & Lake

was the LSWR's delivery agent at Barnstaple and, as he operated several coach services in the area, this was clearly seen by the LSWR as a useful way of collecting traffic for their railway and therefore of benefit to them. Whilst no doubt a useful addition to the transport arrangements of the area, this service in no way met the real long-term needs of the public for either passenger or goods transport.

In 1862, the Okehampton Railway was incorporated to build a line off the North Devon at Coleford (west of Crediton) to Okehampton. In 1863 powers were granted for an extension to Lidford (or Lydford as it is now known). In 1865, the title of the company was changed to the Devon & Cornwall Railway with additional powers for extensions to Bude and to Torrington from Hatherleigh. Okehampton was eventually reached in 1871 with Lidford gaining rails three years later. The powers for the Bude extension lapsed in 1875, but four years later, in 1879, a line to Holsworthy from Meldon Junction, west of Okehampton, was opened, but it was not until 1898 that the last section finally linked Bude to the railway network. About halfway between Meldon Junction and Holsworthy was Halwill and in 1886 this became Halwill Junction with the opening of the line down to Launceston. Almost forty years will elapse before Halwill again features in our narrative.

Difficulties were experienced in raising the necessary capital and further Acts in 1867 and 1869 were needed to keep matters in hand. The latter Act changed the name of the Company yet again to the Bude & Torrington Junction Railway, but the cash required to extend to Torrington could not be raised and thus this part of the line was not built. The route of the Hatherleigh line to Torrington would have followed the valley of the Langtree, which joins the Torridge by Staplevale. The LSWR line was to terminate at Staplevale where it could meet with the northbound line, rather than further up the bed of the old Rolle Canal and nearer to the town itself. As we now know, this was to no avail, the connection to the south from Torrington not materialising until 1925.

Pressure for railway connection was vociferous in Torrington, where a meeting on the subject at the Town Hall was reported in the *Bideford Gazette* of 22nd October 1861. The meeting adopted a resolution that:

"Railway communication with Torrington being essential for the welfare and convenience of its inhabitants, as well as advantageous to its trade and owners of property generally, it was resolved that the following gentlemen, with power to add to their number, be requested to attend as a deputation to confer with members of the Northern Division of the County, and with such railway companies as may be thought advisable, as to the best means to be adopted to expediate (sic) the advantages of railway accommodation of the town and district: - Messrs G. Doe, G. Toms, J.H. Lake, E. Handford, E. Stoneman, and H. Friendship."

Torrington Station and Furzebeam.
Looking down on the station from the edge of the commons, circa 1923. Although not clear, the siding to the left of empty wagons seems to be the Marland line's transfer siding, which ran between two standard gauge sidings. The road up to the town has been realigned a couple of times and now runs to the right of the seat in the foreground.
(Tom Bartlett Postcard Collection, Berrynarbor, EX34 9SE)

A further meeting in Bideford in February 1865 discussed ways of opening up communication with Torrington, Plymouth and the west of Cornwall. Eventually, assisted by considerable lobbying, particularly by the Hon Mark Rolle of Stevenstone House, Torrington – the Lord of the Manor – the Torrington Extension Railway was authorised by Parliament on 6th June 1865, only ten days before the Devon & Cornwall Railway's never-to-be-completed Torrington Extension line was authorised. The line was to be operated by the LSWR as a standard gauge extension from Bideford – the line through Barnstaple to Bideford still being of mixed broad/standard gauge. However the post "mania" years were not a time for capital investment in new minor lines and, with money hard to come by, the LSWR's interest waned fast. They did little to implement the Act and indeed, in 1868, tried to have the Act annulled:

"Under pressure from the shareholders the London and South Western went to Parliament for powers to abandon it; but were firmly withstood by the Hon Mark Rolle, thanks to whose gallant opposition permission to violate the engagement to construct the line was refused."

Parliament twice refused permission to cancel and, in February 1868, the Torrington town council presented a petition against the abandonment. Again Mark Rolle was vociferous in trying to persuade the Company to carry out its obligations, strenuously fighting the case in Parliament and, eventually, in 1869 the LSWR had to bow to the inevitable and with Parliamentary approval for an extension of time, began construction. So strenuously had Mr Rolle fought for construction of the line that Parliament ordered the LSWR to pay his expenses. The idea of a canal owner and major landowner fighting vehemently for a railway to be built on his canal is an amusing one to say the least. It had been reported:

"Mr Rolle would be glad to see the canal superseded by a more useful and convenient mode of transit and communication."

The good people of Torrington were most pleased at this

Stevenstone House, Great Torrington
George Rolle, a lawyer, bought the Stevenstone estate in the 1520s and built himself "a right fair house of brick". This was altered and remodelled in the eighteenth century, but the Hon Mark Rolle rebuilt it completely between 1868 and 1872, as shown in this photograph. Professor Hoskins called it "a villainously ugly house". After Mark Rolle's death, the house was sold and the new owners subsequently demolished much of the building as an economy measure, and partly rebuilt the rest! The estate lands were sold off separately. Resold again, the house was left empty for years until it was opened up as a billet for troops – British and then American – during the WWII. After the war, in the absence of a buyer, it was emptied and left to fall into ruin! Little now remains of this once great building other than part of one of the corner towers, now heavily clad in ivy; although much of the stone was used in the conversion of the old stable block into pretty mews type houses, and the construction of several bungalows in what was the old kitchen garden.
(Tom Bartlett Postcard Collection, Berrynarbor, EX34 9SE)

outcome and the Town Council meeting in May 1868 resolved:

"That the Council feels bound to record their high opinion of the public spirit shown by the Hon Mark Rolle in opposing at his own expense the bill brought into the House of Commons by the London and South Western Railway Company for the abandonment of the Torrington extension, and have great pleasure in offering him their thanks and those of the inhabitants of his liberality. The council also begs to congratulate him on the successful issue of his exertions, which will secure the benefit of railway communication to the town and neighbourhood."

Similar feelings were also expressed to the Right Hon Lord Clinton, and Sir George Stucley, Bart, MP, for:

"...their energetic opposition to the abandonment of this railway, and their attendance before the Parliamentary Committee." and "to J.C. Moore-Stevens, Esq, for the support he has always given to the extension of a railway to this town, and especially for the sacrifice of time and comfort he has made in going three times to London as a witness against the Company's Abandonment Bill at the meetings of the Parliamentary Committee."

(Mr Moore-Stevens was incidentally Gazetted High Sheriff of Devonshire for 1869, so there was some obvious political clout in the area!) It is good to record that Mr Rolle, Lord Clinton and Sir George Stucley all wrote thanking the council for their appreciation.

Construction work on the extension began in May 1870 under the control of W.R. Galbraith, the Company's chief

The Development of Railways - a General View

engineer. The contractor was James Taylor, one of their regular contractors. By February 1871, work was well advanced with the tunnel and viaduct at Landcross being the major works still to be completed. Lt Col Yolland of the Board of Trade carried out an inspection on 7th June 1872 and approved the opening of the new station at Bideford, but refused to accept the rest of the line due to the incompleteness of the works. On his return visit on 12th July, he found matters virtually complete, and his report of the following day noted that only the installation of a crossover at the end of the Torrington platforms was required, although he also made a suggestion regarding a catch point off the turntable and shed road. The required work was put in hand immediately and completed early the following week.

It was thus the following Thursday, 18th July 1872 that the railway finally arrived in Torrington, to the great delight of the populace. The events that followed are best described by reference to the *North Devon Journal* of Thursday, 25th July 1872. In a lengthy article, taking up the whole of page 8, their enthusiastic reporter waxed lyrical:

"The town of Torrington rejoices at length in the advent of the railway as an accomplished fact. For many years the vision of the line had excited its hopes only to trifle with and disappoint them; and there is no doubt that the rail would even yet have been in the dim distance, but for a piece of good luck the inhabitants could hardly have calculated upon, and for the attainment of which they are indebted solely to the exertions of the Hon Mark Rolle. Not that even he is entitled to greater merit than this – that, having in the first place obtained the promise of a boon, which was not the less an advantage to the public because it was also a very great private benefit to himself, he undertook the labour and expense of compelling the railway company to fulfil their engagement when they would have abandoned it, if they might have been permitted."

The article continues with an account of the machinations that preceded the construction of the line and the part that Mark Rolle played in bringing the line eventually to Torrington. The article discusses the merits or otherwise

The Torrington & Marland Light Railway

A busy scene at Torrington station circa 1913, showing the constricted nature of the site and its distance from the town, which lies over the hill to the top left of the picture. The transfer siding of the Torrington and Marland line is to the left of the wagons and brake van seen in the centre of the picture.
(Tom Bartlett Postcard Collection, Berrynarbor, EX34 9SE)

of running the line down the west bank of the Torridge as was done, rather than along the east bank. The climb up to the town from the station generates some comment, but continues:

"As it is, the run down to the line may be accomplished; and if the walk up must perforce be more deliberate, it must be confessed that there is enough in the landscape to beguile the way. The prospect is, in fact, full of beauty. The towering hillsides on the right clothed with sylvan verdure, the river in the vale beneath murmuring along its gentle way, the rich meadows regaling the eye with their greenness, and in the distance the commandingly situate mansion of Cross, (now the residence of the High Sheriff of Devon, J.G. Johnson, Esq, formerly of the worthy Sir Trevor Wheler, Bart, and still more remotely, as some of us recollect, of the recorder of Barnstaple, Thomas Stevens, Esq) embosomed in timber of stately growth, looks down on the quiet and serene depths beneath, and across over upon the ancient borough as if it were its patron saint. Few towns anywhere possess more of real beauty than Torrington."

The report goes on to conjecture that the roads to Barnstaple and Bideford would become far less used, other than by tourists! Continuing now on a matter more close to the main thrust of our story, the Journal's correspondent muses:

"An item of local traffic, which, we imagine will find the line, and which will be likely to expand in its importance, is the article of china clay (sic), found largely in native beds in the neighbourhood of Petrockstowe, six or seven miles to the west, and hitherto carried by the canal – the Rolle canal, now altogether superseded by the line – down to Bideford, and where transhipped off to Staffordshire and other parts, where it is in great request. It was thought some time ago that this traffic would go by carts on to a place of shipment on the Torridge; but believe it is likely the rail will have the benefit of it so far as it can accommodate it. And the thought of this traffic brings again the reflection that the work now accomplished – that of bringing the line to Torrington – cannot in any sense be looked upon as a final one. The expenditure of nearly £100,000 just to save five miles in the local traffic to and from Torrington is altogether

The Development of Railways - a General View

56   1st JUNE to 30th SEPTEMBER 1909, or until further notice.

NORTH DEVON LINE.

FOR SPEED RESTRICTIONS SEE PAGES A, B, C & D.

This is a **Single Line** from **Torrington** to Barnstaple and from **Umberleigh** to **Coppleston**, between which points it is worked under the Regulations for working Single Lines by the Electric **Train Tablet** Block System.

UP TRAINS —WEEK DAYS·

Distance from Torrington. M.C.	STATIONS.	1 Goods C arr. a.m.	1 dep. a.m.	2 Engine. arr. a.m.	2 dep. a.m.	3 Passenger arr. a.m.	3 dep. a.m.	4 Passenger arr. a.m.	4 dep. a.m.	5 Express Passenger July 12th to Septr. 27th inclusive. arr. a.m.	5 dep. a.m.	6 Express Passenger. arr. a.m.	6 dep. a.m.	7 Passenger arr. a.m.	7 dep. a.m.	8 Passenger arr. p.m.	8 dep. p.m.	9 Loco, Coal when required. arr. p.m.	9 dep. p.m.	10 Light Engine. arr. p.m.	10 dep. p.m.
... ...	**Torrington**	...	...	...	7 0	...	7 45	...	9 30	...	10 35	...	11 15	...	1140	...	1210	...	...	...	...
				After No. 1 Down arrs.		After No. 1 Down arrs		After No. 3 Down.		After No. 6 Down.		After No. 7 Down.		After No. 7 Down.		After No. 7 Down.					
5 9	**Bideford (New)**	...	...	7 10		7 54	7 56	9 39	9 42	10 44	10 46	11 24	1127	1149	1150	1219	1221	...	...	...	...
						Cross No. 2 Down.		Cross No 4 Down													
5 49	Bideford (Goods)	...	...	...	...	...	...	...	...	...	...	...	...	...	...	...	...	...	...	A 12 50	
																				After No. 19 Down. 12 58	
7 59	Instow	...	...	7 15		8 1	8 2	9 47	9 48	10 51	10 52	11 32	11 33	11 55	11 56	12 26	12 28	...	...		
											Cross No. 7 Down.						Cross No. 10 Down.					
11 40	Fremington	...	...	7 21		8 9	8 10	9 55	9 56	10 58		11 39		12 3	12 4	12 34		...	12 48	1 3	...
								After No. 5 Down arrs.				After No 9 Down arrs.						After No. 10 Down.			
14 09	**Barnstaple Jct.**	...	5 50	7 26	...	8 15	8 20	10 1	10 5	11 2	11 7	11 43	1148	12 9	...	1238	1243	12 54		...	...
18 38	Chapelton	6 2	6 10			...	8 28	10 13	10 14	...	...	...	...	...	...	...	...	...	...	...	...
20 68	Umberleigh	6 18	6 26			8 33	8 34	10 19	10 20	11 17½		11 58½		...	...	12 53½		1 8		...	...
		After No. 1 Down.				After No. 4 Down.		After No. 6 Down.		After No. 9 Down.		After No. 10 Down.				After No. 10 Town.		After No. 10 Down.			
25 01	Portsmouth Arms	6 40	6 50			8 41	8 42	10 27	10 28	11 23½		12 4½		...	...	12 59½		1 18		...	...
		Cross No. 2 Down.																			
27 72	South Molton Road	6 59	7 33			8 47	8 48	10 33	10 34	11 28½		12 9½		...	...	1 4½	1 5	1 26		...	...
		Cross No. 4 Down.																			
31 67	Eggesford	7 45	8 10			8 55	8 56	10 41	10 42	11 35		12 16		...	...	1 12	1 13	1 36	2 13	...	...
								Cross No. 9 Down.		Cross No. 10 Down.								Cross Nos.11 & 13 Down.			
35 60	Lapford	8 22	8 40			9 3	9 4	10 49	10 50	11 41		12 22		...	...	1 19½		2 24		...	...
																Cross No. 11 Down.					
38 09	Morchard Road	8 50	9 20			9 9	9 11	10 55	10 56	11 45½		12 26½		...	...	1 24		2 34	3 0	...	...
		Shunt for No. 3 Up. Cross No. 6 Down.				Pass No. 1 Up. Cross No. 6 Down.												Cross No. 14 Down. Shunt for No. 12 Up.			
39 60	Coppleston	9 27	9 52	...	...	9 15	9 16	11 0	11 1	11 48½		12 29½		...	...	1 27		3 5		...	...
41 59	Coleford Junction		9 57	...	...	9 19		11 4		11 51		12 32		...	...	1 29½		3 10		...	...
42 56	**Yeoford Junc.**	10 0	10 6	...	...	9 21	9 22	11 6	11 7	11 52		1233½	1235	...	...	1 31	1 43	3 13	3 18	...	...
53 75	**Exeter** (Queen St.)	1053	...	...	...	9 50	...	1132	...	12 11	12 17	12 55	1 0	...	...	2 3	2 10	4 21	...	...	...
225 57	**London** (Waterloo)	...	...	...	...	...	...	...	...	3 37	...	4 40	...	...	...	5 47	...	...	...	...	...

A A Tablet for this Light Engine to be taken from Bideford (New) to Bideford (Goods) by a competent man provided by the Station Master.

C The load of No. 1 Train must not exceed equal to 50 Wagons, two loads coal counting as three.

11

disproportionate to so limited a result. The line must go on further, as everybody must see when he stands and looks around Torrington station. That cannot be a terminus. Where should it be? Where, but beyond – to meet the Devon and Cornwall line at some point – to restore the old and short way of communication between North Devon and Cornwall, and North Devon and Plymouth, now taken by the roundabout route of Exeter. We do not now stay to enquire where the point of junction should be; but that that should be the aim, and that that will be the achievement before many years have passed, we can have no doubt."

The line was opened to traffic on the Thursday of the previous week – Thursday 18th July 1872, and the article described the arrival in Torrington of the first train, the down mail, which was greeted by a "large crowd of townspeople… who raised a large shout of welcome…" Although it was early in the morning (the train was probably the 5.43am off Bideford, due in at 5.55am):

"The crowd remained and became replenished by many additions, as the time drew on for the departure of the morning train, which bore the first freight of passengers and goods going direct from Torrington to – who shall say where? The engine received profuse floral decorations, which served to proclaim festivity, if they could not succeed in converting the ungainly machine into 'a thing of beauty' which will be 'a joy forever' more for what it does than what it looks. The crowd vociferated as the train emerged out of the station, and shout after shout reverberated through the valley as it hastened on its way.

"So each following train of the day – both coming in and going out – was watched with great interest. The day, fortunately, was a fine one and the station kept up an air of gaiety throughout it."

The spectacle of such crowds out so early in the day must have been quite incredible. The air of celebration apparently gets better as the day goes on, for:

"The afternoon was quite a holiday. Many from Bideford and elsewhere came, and hundreds upon hundreds from Torrington went, to make a trial of the new line, all, of course, highly delighted at being driven over it in little over ten minutes, and sometimes less, the timed departures from the two stations being 14 minutes apart."

After discussing the possible provision of an intermediate station, the *Journal* goes on to comment that in view of the fact that the day was such a fine one, it was unfortunate that the people of Torrington could not have made it convenient to have their festivities on that day! Apparently, the forgoing celebrations and rejoicings were purely informal and not organised! Since a great deal of organisation was required by the people of Torrington and

they were not to be rushed into holding their celebration until they were ready, the official opening actually took place the following Wednesday, the 24th July; that is the day after this report appeared in the *Journal*. The *Journal* scribe, who must have been a man of some stamina, continues his report:

"THE FORMAL OPENING took place, as fixed, on Wednesday (yesterday). Most auspiciously, the sun undertook to gladden and to gild all the preparations which local skill and art had elaborated. It was a day long to be remembered in the town of Torrington, and she has entitled herself to the credit of having come out worthily on the occasion. The day, of course, was a high holiday. No less a tribute than the surrender of a day to its honour was due to the great event. From early morning the note of festivity was heard, and as the day drew on the arrivals of company from all parts, and in vehicles and by modes of all kinds, told the people of the town that they would have no lack of sympathetic visitors from far and near to share in the hilarity of their celebration. The first item in the official programme for the day was one which suffered somewhat in its significance from the fact that the line had for some days been actually open and at work. It was felt that there must be a procession, (Author's note: Torrington is still very keen on processions, and manages to have several throughout the course of every year) and whither it should go but to the central place of attraction? What it should do there was not quite so clear; but a procession there must be to the railway, and so there was, and it was made a very attractive feature of the day's proceedings. It was formed, of course, at the Town Hall, and marched thence in order to the Station at the foot of the town, where it awaited the arrival of the forenoon train (eleven o'clock). It came in a few minutes after time, and the spectacle which awaited it was a very lively one. A loud cheer gave forth its welcome to the hundreds from Barnstaple, Bideford and parts more distant, who had been tempted by the fineness of the weather, and the promised gaiety of the day to make trial of the extension to Torrington. The engine was fitted out with floral dress for the occasion. The station and its fine surroundings were lined with hundreds of spectators. The extensive common was dotted in all directions by parties on their holiday best who had come out to witness and to contribute to the universal joyousness. It was to be regretted that circumstances prevented the presence of any of the officials of the London and South Western Railway Company to receive the congratulations of the inhabitants through their worthy chief magistrate. His Worship the Mayor, in his robes, nonetheless made an appropriate speech and the procession then duly reformed and made its way back up the hill to the Town Hall."

The article describes in some detail the make up of the procession – a large party of navvies, the band of the North Devon Hussars, a posse of the Bideford Rifle Volunteer Corps, the town officers, representatives of the professional and private gentlemen and all the tradesmen. The local fire engine drawn by "four fine greys with postilions" was followed by representatives of the local court of Foresters and Castle Lodge. Then came a long procession of representatives of the trades and industries of the town. Included in this was "a carriage drawn by two greys, of which the occupants were six young women in graceful holiday attire, who, as they went along, were busily working at their sewing machines, representative of their daily employment at Messrs Vaughan's gloving factory." Agricultural representation then followed. Several triumphal arches of evergreens had been erected over the road and floral decorations were out in abundance, with almost every house, public house and shop being decorated in some way. A dinner was provided at one o'clock for the "working class and poor" men of the area, in the covered marketplace (the pannier market) where some 600 were duly fed and watered.

"Dinner being over, the Town Crier gave public notice that sports would immediately commence on Castle Hill; and to Castle Hill therefore the crowds began to repair. Such crowds have scarcely ever before been seen in Torrington. Thousands upon thousands were attracted to the hill – many to behold the rustic sports improvised for the occasion, but more to enjoy the scenery commanded from that delightful spot – one of the most charming in Devonshire."

After the sports, the women and children were entertained to tea, between 1,600 and 1,700 assembling in three sittings in the Market House! Among the ladies listed as helping with this vast undertaking was a Miss Hole, who may well have been Sarah Honoria Hole, (who appears in a later chapter). It would seem that the town's capacity to feed vast numbers of people in a short space of time was undiminished, for:

"In the evening, at six o'clock, a large party of gentlemen sat down to a very sumptuous banquet in the Town Hall, to which the Mayor and Town Council had bidden a great number of distinguished guests. Speeches were many, loyal and lavish and included one from the Rev J Brierly who, as a

relative newcomer to the town, 'looked upon the Torrington Extension Railway as one of a series of works bringing political, religious, social, and intellectual liberty to all parts of the land.' (Applause)."

The Chairman – the Mayor of Torrington, N. Chapple Esq, proposed what seems to have been the main toast of the evening, to the Hon Mark Rolle for all he had done for the poor of the area, for the donation of the fountain in the market place and for the railway ("loud and prolonged cheers"). In his reply to the toast, Mr Rolle said "he was going to predict that the station at Torrington would not long remain the terminus, and that before many years they would see Torrington connected with the western ports of Bideford and Plymouth by rail." After all this, the company took to the dance floor, and "hundreds danced to a late – if not rather an early – hour".

The absence of any representatives of the LSW Railway Company was noted in the speeches – an impending half-yearly General Meeting was given as the reason – but in all probability the Company was still smarting from having to spend £100,000 (25% over the original estimate of £80,000) on a line it did not really want. It was obvious that the good folk of Torrington would not let matters rest here, as we saw from the reported speeches, and every available opportunity was taken to publicly praise the railway and press for its extension.

The opening of the Holsworthy line in 1879 was greeted locally with great enthusiasm and the *North Devon Journal* carried a lengthy report of the opening celebrations in its issue of 23rd January 1879.

With the railway now as near as Halwill, local feeling in Torrington was increasingly that the LSWR's line from Torrington should be extended southwards as soon as possible, to serve the Marland Brick and Clay Works which was still several miles away from a railhead, and to provide a through link to Plymouth. The new Torrington station had been designed to easily convert to a through station but, clearly, the LSWR were in no mood to even discuss the matter and it would be for local initiative to bring rails south.

Extract from 1914 Public Time Table.

High Street, Torrington in about 1901/2.
Other than the usual alteration to shop fronts, the buildings have changed little over the years. The last building on the right hand side, with the twin white fronted gables, is the Black Horse Inn. This is one of the oldest buildings in the town and was the headquarters of the Royalist General Lord Hopton at the start of the Civil War Battle of Torrington in 1646. The rather ornate structure in the centre of the picture, immediately behind the little girl second on the left, is a fountain donated to the town by the Hon Mark Rolle in 1870.
(Tom Bartlett Postcard Collection, Berrynarbor, EX34 9SE)

Chapter 2

DEVONSHIRE IN THE NINETEENTH CENTURY

The county of Devon, or Devonshire, occupies the widest part of the southwest peninsula of England and geographically it is the third largest county in England after Yorkshire and Lincolnshire. It shares with Cornwall and Kent the distinction of having both a north and south coast. The county is divided geologically into two distinct areas by the southern end of the fault line which runs down England from the River Tees to the River Exe: to the south-east lie the newer red rocks of the Permian and Triassic periods; to the west, the older granite, sandstone and limestone with the vast culm measures of impure anthracite in central and west Devon. Somerset, to the east, provides most of the link between Devon and Cornwall (Dorset juts in a little in the south) and the rest of England in the form of a relatively narrow strip of land between Lyme Regis in the south and the mouth of the River Parrett in the north. In the north of this narrow strip are the Somerset Levels, a low-lying flood plain much prone to heavy flooding in the winter months in the nineteenth century, as they still are in the twenty first century! After them, sprawling like wild animals waiting in ambush for an unwary victim, lie the Quantock Hills almost directly ahead, with the Brendon Hills just behind running into the mass of Exmoor. A little to the south are the Blackdown Hills blocking the route in that direction.

The early traveller thus initially found his route west almost blocked, and for centuries the only reasonable paths through to Devon have been the gap between the Brendon and Blackdown Hills to the north, and through the valley of the Axe to the south. Thus the traveller had to pass through Axminster and on to Exeter, or through Taunton. Once through either of these, the huge granite mass of Dartmoor then forced a turn either south along a coastal route, or to the north and across Mid Devon. In the early days of travel, when the horse was the only alternative to two feet, these were the only routes to or from the southwest. Where roads existed in anything like recognisable form, they varied from very rough tracks to occasionally maintained rough roads. It was not until the middle of the nineteenth century that the work of Telford and McAdam began to create roads that were half worthy of the name. Goods traffic – carried by packhorse from early days until into the nineteenth century – was largely at the mercy of the weather; a good downpour would turn a "major" route into an impassable sea of mud.

Not all transport was by land, and much goods traffic used the rivers to connect to coastal shipping routes, which often provided as quick a journey as the apparently more direct land route. It was also possible to carry greater cargoes by river and sea than by land. Typically, a coaster would carry fifty or more tons, which would require several hundred packhorses or a dozen large wagons on the roads. However,

by the seventeenth century, road based carrier services had developed from such centres as Exeter, Barnstaple, Tiverton and Bampton to London, and by 1722 goods from London could be in Exeter in about six days.

The intrepid traveller (and intrepid he must have been) venturing very far from home would either be on horseback or, if his journey was further afield, on one of the new passenger carrying coach services – the stagecoach, which came into being after the middle of the seventeenth century. These of course were only for the "well to do" – the gentry or upper classes. The lower classes, if they had the need to travel, would use one of the goods carrying stage-wagons. Labourers would often have to walk to work and this in many cases could involve a journey of five miles or more each way. It must be noted that at this time only the very well off could afford to travel, or indeed, would have the need so to do. Even when the railways first started operating, they were originally designed for carriage of goods and it was almost as an afterthought that provision was made for passengers. Then it was only "first class" passengers who were really catered for; the class divides were well maintained by the fledgling railway companies.

The first of the stage coaches to enter Devon was in 1658, when the London to Exeter stage took four days for the journey at probably not more than an average of three miles per hour. By 1828 the time for the journey had been slashed to less than twenty hours! The rapid improvement in journey times, and the greater ease of use of the road system as it then existed, was largely due to the formation of Turnpike Trusts from about 1700. Previously, the 1555 Highways Act had placed the responsibility for roads on the local parishes, which were expected to maintain them using unpaid labour under unpaid supervision. Hence little, if any, repair work was done and certainly no improvements. The Turnpike Trusts however, which were formed locally by landowners, merchants and other interested parties, took over the upkeep and maintenance of a given stretch of road in return for the right to levy a toll on users. The rights to operate the Trusts were auctioned annually and it was through the operation of these Trusts that the standards of roads rose dramatically, bringing major improvements in conditions of travel. The first Trusts in Devon were formed in Exeter, Honiton and Axminster in 1753 with Tiverton, Okehampton and Barnstaple following in 1757, 1760 and 1763. It was not until 1765 that the Great Torrington Trust was formed under an Act of 1759.

With its heavily indented coastline, Devon has many river valleys running roughly north and south, which also impeded the passage of the road traveller. Bridges and ferries were to be found in some places in earlier days, but these were few and far between and thus roads or tracks had to meander along and round valleys adding many miles to journeys. Hence in the early days, the river and coastal vessel trade could often be more economical both in terms of speed and cost. Whilst the development of the long-distance carrier linking towns and cities was important, the local or country-carrier also developed at the same time. These carriers performed a much wider function than merely moving goods from A to B. They delivered farm produce to the nearby town, collected orders in the town for the rural community, and provided the only means of public transport and later, in areas poorly served by the railways, they delivered goods from the railhead to the outlying areas.

Apart from the Exeter Ship Canal, begun in 1564, canals did not make an appearance until the "canal mania" of the 1790s although, because of the number of rivers and ports in the county, there were far fewer proposed for Devon than elsewhere. The Stover or Teigngrace Canal was completed in 1794 connecting the clay and lignite deposits at Bovey Tracey to the Teign at Newton Abbott. This canal was increased in importance in 1820 when George Templar built an eight and a half mile tramway from his quarries near Hay Tor to Ventiford on the Stover Canal. The short-lived Grand Western Canal was authorised in 1796 to link Devon to the national canal system, but by 1820 it had only been opened from Tiverton to Burlescombe, although later it was extended via Wellington to Taunton. The Great Western Railway bought it in 1865 and it was then largely abandoned. A short canal from Tavistock to Morwellham Quay on the Tamar opened in 1817 bringing slate and mineral ores from Mill Hill quarries. The connection of Tavistock to the railway network in 1892 and the general decline in mining at the same time ensured that the canal did not see out the century. The Bude – Holsworthy Canal had been authorised in 1819, but did not open until 1826. It was built to handle sea sand traffic to the inland parts of the county, and was originally intended to reach Okehampton, but it only lasted until about 1885. It reopened for a while in the late 1890s to assist in the carriage of materials for the Holsworthy – Bude railway.

During the 1790s, several other canals were proposed for the area but never materialised, including Barnstaple to Cowley Bridge, Exeter linking the Taw and the Exe, and very relevantly to this study, one from Wear Giffard on the Torridge to run through Peters Marland, Sheepwash and Hatherleigh to Okehampton, where it would have joined another from Exeter to Crediton. Had this latter venture been successful, how much different might have been our story, and different indeed the fortunes of the inhabitants and merchants of the area. A canal from Wear Giffard to Okehampton would have opened up the hinterland of North Devon much earlier and would without doubt have changed the map of railway development in the area and brought it about earlier. A viable canal system was always an object of attack for the new railway companies and this route would surely have been an early target for purchase and conversion to rail. It could thus be argued that main line railways would

have been operating in this part of Devon and providing a seamless link to the rest of the country by the middle of the nineteenth century, thus increasing the trade and prosperity of the region beyond measure.

Great Torrington

Situated some six miles south south-east of Bideford in the lovely North Devon countryside, Great Torrington "is one of the most finely sited towns in Devon, on the top of a cliff rising steeply from the meadows of the Torridge." So said Professor W.G. Hoskins in his 1954 *Survey of England* volume on Devon. A sixteenth century traveller described it as "a great large Towne, and standith on the brow of an Hille and hath a three faire Streates Yn it, and a good Market every weke, and ons a Yere upon St. Michael's day, the best Fayr in al those Quarters". Clearly a town of some importance, it was a centre for the wool trade of the area and although not a port, was only two miles or so from the navigable head of the River Torridge. White's Directory of 1878 describes Great Torrington as "a parish, well built market town, and ancient borough, pleasantly seated on a bold eminence on the north-east side of the picturesque valley of the river Torridge". Harrod's Directory for the same year advises, "the air is healthy and salubrious."

The history of Great Torrington can be traced back to the 1086 Devonshire Doomsday Survey. Fortifications of some sort were built here long ago, but these were destroyed by Royal command in 1228. In the fourteenth century Richard de Merton built a castle and keep overlooking the river, and in 1554 the town became a charter borough. During the Civil War, Torrington was the site of one of the last great battles between Royalists and Parliamentarians. In February 1646 the parish church, which was being used as a powder store, blew up killing some 200 Royalist soldiers held prisoner by the Parliamentarians. This signalled the end for Charles I, for the Parliamentarians under Lord Fairfax soon defeated the Royalist forces under Lord Hopton thus effectively ending the King's war in the west. Torrington has not been without it's notable citizens and visitors, and has shared in Devon's historical past. The town was a municipal borough, market and union town, parish, petty sessional division and county court district. The manor and borough of Torrington belonged to the Hon Mark George Kerr Trefusis Rolle of Stevenstone House. The population of the town increased during the nineteenth century, from 2,044 in 1801, to 3,298 in 1861, 3,436 in 1891 with a brief peak to 3,529 in 1871.

A fairly diverse range of small industries could be found in the area. The cloth trade had been active in Torrington for centuries, tucking mills being well established along the Torridge centred on the Weare Giffard and Torrington area. Glove making was prominent in the town since the fifteenth century and this overtook the wool trade in importance during the nineteenth century, with the production of silk gloves being the town's speciality. Such was the size of the trade that in the 1880s, one factory alone was employing over 600

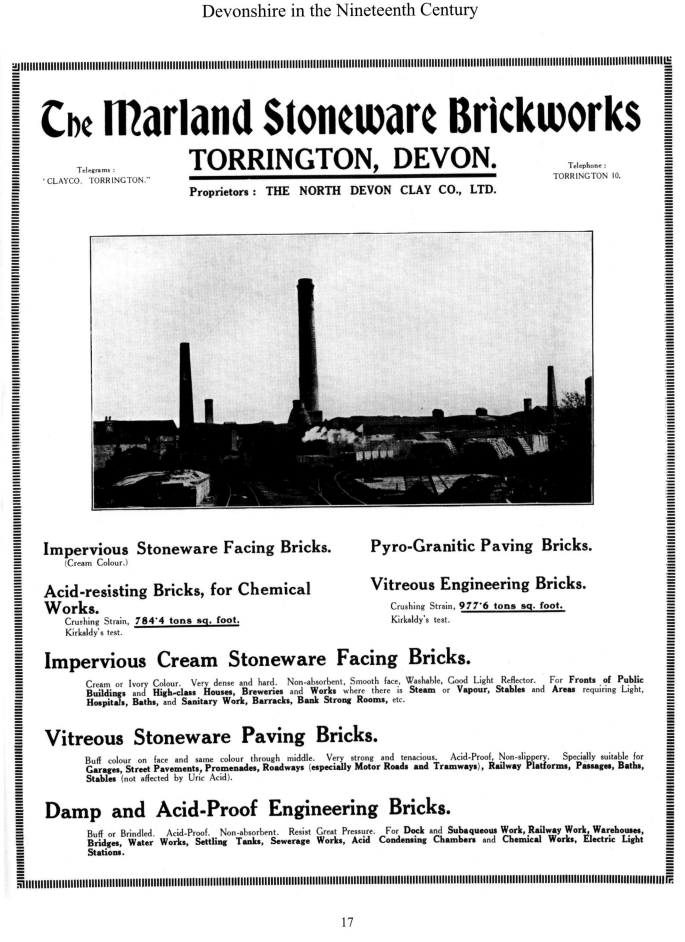

The Marland Stoneware Brickworks
TORRINGTON, DEVON.

Telegrams :
"CLAYCO, TORRINGTON."

Telephone :
TORRINGTON 10.

Proprietors : THE NORTH DEVON CLAY CO., LTD.

Impervious Stoneware Facing Bricks.
(Cream Colour.)

Acid-resisting Bricks, for Chemical Works.
Crushing Strain, **784·4 tons sq. foot.**
Kirkaldy's test.

Pyro-Granitic Paving Bricks.

Vitreous Engineering Bricks.
Crushing Strain, **977·6 tons sq. foot.**
Kirkaldy's test.

Impervious Cream Stoneware Facing Bricks.

Cream or Ivory Colour. Very dense and hard. Non-absorbent, Smooth face, Washable, Good Light Reflector. For **Fronts of Public Buildings** and **High-class Houses, Breweries** and **Works** where there is **Steam** or **Vapour, Stables** and **Areas** requiring Light, **Hospitals, Baths,** and **Sanitary Work, Barracks, Bank Strong Rooms,** etc.

Vitreous Stoneware Paving Bricks.

Buff colour on face and same colour through middle. Very strong and tenacious. Acid-Proof, Non-slippery. Specially suitable for **Garages, Street Pavements, Promenades, Roadways (especially Motor Roads and Tramways), Railway Platforms, Passages, Baths, Stables** (not affected by Uric Acid).

Damp and Acid-Proof Engineering Bricks.

Buff or Brindled. Acid-Proof. Non-absorbent. Resist Great Pressure. For **Dock** and **Subaqueous Work, Railway Work, Warehouses, Bridges, Water Works, Settling Tanks, Sewerage Works, Acid Condensing Chambers** and **Chemical Works, Electric Light Stations.**

The Clay Pits

Several views of the clay workings, showing some of the methods used for cutting and moving the clay from the pit to the works during the period 1930–1940:

Above: A general view of the opencast mine, showing men cutting the clay into 28lb cubes or "balls". This view shows the scale of operations and lack of mechanisation.

Left: Looking up the side of the mine, with men cutting clay back from the side of the mine. Note the truck on "railway" to carry the balls up to the top of the mine, and the steps and handrail for the men behind the track.

Opposite page: A busy scene showing the use of pneumatic cutters, dated 1936–1938.

(All The Beaford Archive)

factory and outworkers. Four tanneries were active in the town and flour milling was also a staple trade. In 1874 the Torridge Vale Butter factory began operation in the old Rolle Canal Company's stores at the lower end of the town. This was to develop into Dairy Crest's large creamery, which sadly was to close in 1993 with the loss of many jobs.

There was a weekly market, and Cattle Fairs were held on 4th May, 5th July, and 10th October with a Grand Cattle Market on the third Saturday in March. The major hotels in the town offered free fishing "on 7 miles of preserved waters" to all their guests. The trout fishing on the Torridge was apparently excellent! In the late nineteenth century the town was also well protected from invasion, for stationed there were A Squadron Royal North Devon Yeomanry Cavalry (Hussars) and F Company of the 4th Volunteer Battalion, Devonshire Regiment, with a Drill Hall and Armoury situated in Calf Street. In 1801 the town was described as "rich, populous and spirited"! Hoskins did not think any of those adjectives very appropriate in 1954, but today the town is being revitalised and Great Torrington is now in the process of claiming them back!

The Clay Moors

The clay from the North Devon area is known as ball clay. It is a finer clay than the better known china clay, with smaller particles that stick together very easily making the clay better to work and mould. Both ball and china clays tend to be used in "white" pottery, the ball clay giving the strength and the china clay the whiteness. Ball clay is much rarer than china clay, and was formed when sediment was washed away from higher ground and was deposited in freshwater lakes and basins. The North Devon deposits were formed some 30 million years ago from material originating in the granite rocks of Dartmoor and, whilst deposits are found in the area around Barnstaple and Bideford, the far greater is that which is trapped in a natural basin, probably the bed of an old lake, in the Peters Marland and Meeth districts south of Torrington. The area lies on a geological fault line, which runs north west to south east from Sticklepath to Lustleigh. The word "Marland" is the Old English word for clay and the Oxford Dictionary gives "land on a lake" as a definition for Peters Marland, which is probably how the area came to be named. The ball clay of the Marland field is of great purity and

"Peter" and "Mary" at the works.
An interesting scene at the works, probably prior to World War I, with a group of men having either just arrived for work, or about to leave for home. The train engine is "Peter", with "Mary" standing alongside. (The National Railway Museum)

strength with a high resistance to acids which make it suitable for a wide range of purposes, such as domestic pottery and earthenware, stoneware pottery, crucibles used in the chemical industry, clay pipes, paper making, and bricks.

Mining was originally carried out in shafts dug into the ground, but by November 1877 these had all been filled in and the clay was being extracted from pits. The name "ball" clay comes from the way in which it was mined in opencast mines and cut out in rough 9-inch cubes or balls weighing about 30 to 35 pounds. The balls of clay were cut manually with a tool known as a pit spade. The clay was cut in steps and men known as Long Scorers made the longitudinal cuts with the pit spade. There would be several of these working at once, some feet away from each other and each cutting the line behind his fellow worker. They would thus form a diagonal line. At the same time "Dirters" would be making the cross cuts, at 90 degrees to the first cuts, also working in a diagonal line. This would produce the square shaped ball outline that was removed by "Diggers", who undercut the ball releasing it from the ground. "Sliders" using a wooden pole with a metal spike known as a prog tool performed the final operation of sliding the ball along to the point where it was loaded onto the tub or skip. The liberal use of water assisted this operation. The tub was then hauled up the side of the pit on rails by a winding engine located at the top, where it was emptied into the waiting railway wagon. The winch man was known as the top man because he worked "up top".

I am indebted to Mr Maurice Dowson of Torrington, a former miner at the clay works during the period following the Second World War, for much of this information. Mr Dowson thinks that the clay was actually called blue ball clay. The wages for the men, according to Mr Dowson's memory, were: Long Scorer, 4½d per hour; Dirter, 4¼d per hour; Digger, 5d per hour.

In later years, as the original pits became worked out, mining was again being carried out in shafts or "drifts", which ran down into the ground at a shallow angle. From these shafts, horizontal passages led off from where the clay was extracted using only hand tools. Each of the clay mines was worked by a group of four miners, in two pairs. One of the four was regarded as the senior man. The clay was dug by hand originally, although compressed air spades weighing some 37lbs were introduced later, and the clay loaded into small tubs running on a narrow gauge track laid down by the miners themselves. They were paid on a piecework basis and expected to shift sixteen tons of clay a day per group (that is, four tons each). They started work at 7.00am and finished when the sixteen tons had been loaded. If it took all day, it took all day! In reality they usually finished by about 2.00pm. At the time Maurice Dowson was employed at the clay works, the basic pay of a labourer was £3.10.0d per week with a miner getting £6.8.0d per week.

In those days, the 3ft gauge main line was gone, but the clay works end of it still operated in the clay fields. The railway was used to transport the men to their mines, which could be two or three miles from the main works, in the workmen's trucks which were known as "shanties" (as shown on page 62). After the men had knocked off (apparently from the practise of coal miners who had just finished work, knocking the metal end off their pickaxe so that it could be re-sharpened for use the following morning) the locomotive would spend the hours until finishing time at 5.00pm distributing empty wagons to each pit head ready for the next morning. On the occasion when a second shift was working, this operation would not take place until early evening, the loco crew having to work the extra hours. The work was very hot and arduous and to quench their thirst the men took a quart (two pints) beer bottle full of cold tea with them. This had to last the whole shift, but the experienced men did not always need to drink all their tea!

The railway out in the clay field was quite temporary and moved as new mines were sunk and others abandoned. Sleepers cut at the works were dropped down on the ground under the supervision of a foreman, and rails offloaded from wagons and dropped down onto the sleepers. These were roughly spiked directly onto the sleepers and joined together with fishplates. The ground was often uneven and gaps would be left under the track in places. This would be filled in with broken brick and soil offloaded from other wagons. During the 1930s, compressed air spades were introduced to improve efficiency. As these weighed about 50lb they must have been a mixed blessing to the men using them. Mechanical power also began to be introduced in the open pits and for loading the railway wagons. Electricity was brought on to the site in 1936 and was used throughout the works and in the mines.

The history of clay extraction goes back hundreds of years in Devon and it is believed that clay was first extracted from the Marland Clay field as long ago as the seventeenth century. Potteries naturally appeared over the years near to the various clay fields, but mostly near the coast or the river Torridge. Records exist of a potter working in Taddiport on the outskirts of Torrington in 1643. He was probably using clay from Peters Marland as Taddiport was on the road from there to Torrington. Bideford was at one time one of the largest ports in Britain and much clay was exported from here over the years. In the period 1654-1655, William and Jasper Greening – both ships' masters – were carrying tobacco-pipe clay to Gloucester and also sending clay elsewhere on other ships. It would seem likely that they had interests in the clay deposits of Peters Marland and certainly by 1692 the family clearly owned part of the clay moors for these were mentioned in the will of one John Greening. In view of the importance of Weare Giffard in the matter of transport, it is interesting to see that Jasper Greening went to live there in 1660. The lack of decent roads ensured that most of the clay came from close at hand and the Marland clay deposits could not be fully exploited. In the early days of the mines, transport was simply governed by the amount that a pack animal could carry. It has been estimated that twelve horses would have been needed to carry one ton of clay.

It was in 1845 that we learn that George Braginton, the

A mechanical shredder being loaded by hand from one of the wagons that has brought the cut clay in from the clay fields. Piles of shredded clay are to be seen on the right, awaiting loading for despatch.
(The Ball Clay Heritage Society)

son Richard Braginton, who had been a Steward of the Rolle Estate for some 40 years, was one of the occupiers of the part of the Marland clay site. He was a prominent local figure, being owner of a local bank and a former Mayor of Torrington. By 1862 at least, his company was running the Annery Pottery at Weare Giffard (originally set up in about 1849) under the name of North Devon Pottery. This was producing domestic pottery, mainly drainage pipes. Also involved in the clay business was Lord Clinton, another prominent landowner, who was extracting clay from nearby Bury Moor by the 1850s. Marriage connections transferred this ownership to the Wren family, and by 1875 William Adderley Barton Wren, JP was the owner of the Marland site. Clay Moor, known previously as Greenings Moor, Grange Moor and Marland Moor made up most of the site, although locally the names varied, as they still do. The Holwill family played a very important role in the development of the Peters

Marland clay operation and of the birth and growth of the Torrington & Marland Railway, and it is worth a reminder here that both of Frederick Holwill's sons, Henry and Eustace, and Eustace's son, E.A. Holwill all played a role in the story.

Names of the personalities involved also change frequently, as we shall see, and sometimes it is a little difficult to keep track of who was who – especially when the same company was called different names at the same time. However, by 1878, the Marland Brick & Tile Works was in operation with Frederick Holwill as works manager. On 12th December 1879, the Marland Brick & Clays Works Ltd was incorporated, and this firm leased the works buildings, kilns and pits from Wren under a 60-year lease. Frederick Holwill was in place as manager.

In the early 1880s, J.W. Ludlam took over the brick making operation, with J.M. Limpus as works manager.

August 1880 saw Wren taking over the North Devon Pottery for £1,687 from the then owner Eliza Maxwell and installing Charles Maxwell as Clay Works Manager – presumably the object of the whole exercise. As an aside, the North Devon Pottery Company was an exhibitor at the 1851 Great Exhibition and won a medal and certificate for their wares. Henry Holwill was to take his place as Works Manager in 1883 at the tender age of 17. Wren was still apparently trading in his own name during 1887/88, probably in clay only. As a portent of how matters would develop many years later, it was on 26th September 1882 that the Marland Brick & Clay Works entered into a 5 year agreement to sell clay to Messrs Watts, Blake Bearne & Co of Newton Abbot and their co-partners, the Devon & Courtenay Clay Co also of Newton Abbot. The Marland Brick & Clay Works Ltd was wound up on 24th January 1888, and on 8th September 1891 another change of name in the main operation took place, this time to the Marland North Devon Brick Company Ltd.

In 1891 another change of control took place when a Manchester brick manufacturer, one William Lawton leased the brick works. The following year, however, Lawton passed the lease to the Marland North Devon Brick Company Ltd, which had been incorporated on 8th September 1891. This company had been given a 5-year lease on the brick works only by Wren, who agreed to carry their products on his railway. By 1893, J.M. Limpus had left and was to be found at Candy & Co of Bovey Tracey, a South Devon clay operation. 1892 also saw Lord Clinton leasing Bury Moor and Clay Moor to the new company. In December 1892, Wren leased all the moors, works and railway to Henry and Eustace Holwill. By now the railway had been extended to clay workings on Bury Moor. The Holwills then set up the North Devon Clay Company Ltd (NDCC), incorporated on 20th May 1893 to carry on the business, with Eustace as Managing Director and Henry as Works Manager. The Articles of Association included in the business description "clay mining and manufacture, general and agricultural dealers and general carriers". The NDCC took over the business of the Marland North Devon Brick Company in January 1894 so that everything was now in the hands of NDCC Ltd. Interestingly, Eustace Holwill retired as Managing Director in June 1894 to move a few miles down the road to take over as Managing Director of the new clay operation at Meeth, as we shall see later in our story. Wren was to die on 26th January 1893 and his two spinster sisters inherited his estate. They leased the site to NDCC in 1893, selling the freehold to the NDCC in 1904.

Henry Holwill died in 1925, and John Sillifant succeeded him until 1936, when he retired. Henry's nephew, E.A. Holwill, then took his place as General Manager. In 1942, a landslip cut off supplies of clay to the brick works and the works was closed. The buildings were requisitioned as a Ministry of Supply storage depot and, whilst under government control, the buildings were destroyed by fire in 1944. The site was cleared after the war for expansion of the clay operations. In 1962, the company set up marketing links with Watts, Blake, Bearne & Co Ltd (WBB) of Newton Abbott, and in 1967 WBB bought a major stake in the company. The following year the whole of the share capital was bought, and control of the whole operation moved to the South Devon Company. The whole operation was soon to change completely; underground mining was completely replaced by opencast pits in 1969 and the following year the narrow gauge railway system was replaced by motor vehicles. Extraction nowadays however is in two huge opencast quarries, entirely by mechanical means and road transport moves the clay around the site, over the local country roads, and so to the ports.

Table 2 shows Clay and brick production figures between 1883 and 1980. Note that the figures have been compiled from various sources and are only given as a guide to activity during the period.

Table 2. Clay and brick production figures		
Year	**Clay (tons per annum)**	**Bricks**
1883	1 200 (monthly)	
1889		25 000 daily
1990	10 000	
1900	15 000	
1901		2.8 million
1905	Over 20 000	
1923	30 000	3.5 million
1925		2.0 million
Early 1930s	1	3.0 million
Circa 1942	30 000	
1967	35 000	
1980	100 000	
2001		

1. Sales of clay apparently dropped during the thirties, whilst brick sales increased, thus reversing a trend in the opposite direction during the first half of the century. However, the First World War of course hit the overseas trade and sales dropped accordingly.

Local Transport

As was discussed earlier, transport in North Devon in the seventeenth and eighteenth centuries was difficult, dangerous and time-consuming. As an example, a journey by carriers cart from Bideford to Bude, some 26 miles, took one full day. The advent of the Turnpike Trusts and the ensuing upgrading of some roads had improved matters, but it was still a difficult area for travel, particularly for the movement of goods. The River Torridge was navigable as far as Weare Giffard and this was used for bulk commodities, such as coal and limestone, which were then "packed" by horse the rest of

The Torrington & Marland Light Railway

A fascinating view of the pitheads, showing the railway with some very interesting pointwork, which was probably taken in the 1890s. The light construction of the line in the clay fields enabled it to be moved quite easily as the need arose. (The Ball Clay Heritage Society)

the way. In the other direction of course, clay and other local products had to be packed as far as Weare Giffard for loading onto barges for onwards transhipment. The transport needs of the people of Torrington appear to have been met by several local carriers: daily services (by horse drawn cart or carriage) to Bideford and Crediton; thrice weekly to Umberleigh; and weekly to Plymouth. The latter left on Tuesdays and returned on the Saturday. After the extension of the railway to Torrington in 1872, White's Directory advised, "two omnibuses, in connection with the principal hotels, meet all the trains." These of course were horse-drawn vehicles and one could sympathise with the poor horses labouring on the hill up from the station to the town. Even today's modern lorries struggle with the gradient

The question of a canal for the area was first raised by local landowner and dignitary Denys Rolle, "to take into consideration the propriety of carrying a canal from some navigable part of the Torridge above Bideford Bridge to Torrington, and to communicate with some or one of the intended canals in this county". Denys Rolle believed that,

using tub-boats and inclined planes, canals could be built high up on the cheap land of hillsides and away from the fertile river valleys, thus reducing the costs of such projects. However, nothing further was done on this matter at that time. In 1810 the noted canal engineer, James Green, had been attempting to survey a route for a canal on the north-eastern side of the Torridge but failed to produce a viable proposal, although Parliamentary notice had been given that the matter was under review. Green, the son of a Birmingham civil engineer, had come to Devon whilst working for John Rennie, the great engineer, and had settled in the county setting up work on his own account. He had been appointed County Bridge Surveyor for Devon in 1808, but continued to work on his own account carrying out extensive works on the Exeter Canal between 1820 and 1832.

However the Torrington area was not forgotten, for in 1823 Lord John Rolle, Denys Rolle's son, of Stevenstone House on the outskirts of Torrington, commissioned Green to build a new canal to link the town with the River Torridge. This was to run some 6 miles from the Torridge near Weare

Giffard to a new gristmill about a mile beyond Great Torrington to the south-east of the town. The Beam Aqueduct was the great constructional feature of the canal and the first stone of this was laid by the Right Honourable John Lord Rolle on 11ᵗʰ August 1824, "in the presence of the Mayor, Corporation and Feoffees of Great Torrington and other persons assembled to witness the commencement of the Canal undertaken at the sole expense of his Lordship". The occasion was clearly one of great jollity to all with the exception of one John Hopgood, who was wounded in the arm by a bursting canon on Furzebeam Hill in Torrington. The Stevenstone (Rolle estate office) accounts show that Mr Caddy the surgeon was paid £12 2s 6d in January the following year for attending to the unfortunate man. The following August, Hopgood himself was awarded "One year's allowance in consequence of the wound…." amounting to £5. The huge disparity in the two figures is of interest, but to be fair to Lord Rolle, the accounts also include a mention of "wine and Porter had for Mr Hopgood" within the entry of settling His Lordship's Mess Bill for the year at the Globe Inn in Torrington. This latter totalled £16 2s ½d so it would seem that His Lordship was considerate of servants, even though we cannot know whether Hopgood was actually at work at the time of his accident.

Opened in 1827 at an estimated cost to Lord Rolle of some £45,000, the canal started with a lock and basin on the western bank of the Torridge some 2 miles upstream from Bideford Bridge and then ran past the Annery lime kilns. From here, an inclined plane, powered by a waterwheel, raised the canal by means of two semi-balanced tubs and the canal then crossed over to the east bank of the river by the magnificent Beam Aqueduct. Following the track of the river, past the lime kilns at Taddiport, the canal then passed the warehouses and offices at the bottom of Mill Street, skirted the southern side of Great Torrington perched high above, to terminate at New Manor Mill. The crenellated mill was built alongside the canal basin and replaced the old manor flour mill near Mill Street. A new road and bridge over both road and canal were built later, opening in 1843; a year after Lord Rolle had died. Interestingly, His Lordship had not applied for either planning permission or an Act of Parliament to build his canal, and the position was not regularised until a retrospective Act was passed in 1836. No doubt today's bureaucrats would have made him fill it in and reapply for permission!

In about 1828, at about the time the canal was being constructed, the Turnpike Trust commenced the building and upgrading of what is now the present A386 road along the west bank of the river valley from Landcross to Torrington. At this time, the Bideford to Torrington road ran across country to Summerhill and over the River Yeo to meet what is now the A388 Bideford to Holsworthy road as far as Monkleigh. From there it ran to Plumpers Bridge and down to the Rakeham Toll House, over the Torridge by way of Rothern Bridge and up the Commons to the Old Bowling Green on the outskirts of Torrington. The new road ran just above the canal for much of its journey and its completion made the journey from Torrington to Bideford much less tortuous. The other route to Torrington from Bideford ran to the east of the Torridge on a somewhat more direct, but

The Rolle Canal, looking south towards Taddiport on the outskirts of Torrington. The view is dated 1876 and is therefore after the railway had been extended from Bideford to Torrington, but before this southern end of the canal had been filled in to form the Rolle Road. The canal continued behind the photographer, following the river to the Town Mills. In the middle distance, Taddiport Bridge can be seen over the River Torridge with Taddiport village itself lying on the far banks of the river. Taddiport was originally founded in the Middle Ages as a leper colony. The old road is now a pleasant riverside walk.
(The Beaford Archive)

circuitous, route. The present Station Hill, from the site of the railway station up to the town, is a 1969 realignment, the previous road running more to the north-west through, rather than skirting, the Commons. That in its turn had been realigned sometime during the period 1859–1865, probably to join up with New Street as part of the Turnpike developments at that time.

A shipyard, known as "Sea Lock", was established on the Torridge by the canal basin and was operating even before the canal opened. The first ship to be launched was in 1827. This was a 98 ton schooner, named The Louisa after Lord Rolle's wife, but soon changed to The Lady Rolle. (Probably use of the first name was thought to be a little presumptuous!) Maritime superstition has it that changing a ship's name is unlucky and so it proved for the little Louisa as she was lost with all hands some thirty years later. The 105 ton The Lord Rolle was the fifth vessel to be launched from the yard. These first five were all registered to William Tardrew of Annery House who was the managing shareholder of the Rolle Canal Company. The shipbuilders operating the yard seem to have changed over the years; William Hutchings is quoted at the first involved and the name of Thomas Saunders is credited with the construction of the Margaret in 1835. This ship was a seasoned traveller by all accounts, trading as far as North America, the Mediterranean and the West Indies. During its short life the yard turned out three-masted schooners for the Newfoundland trade as well as vessels for use in the Mediterranean. The largest vessel to leave the yard was the Sedwell Jane, a 200 ton three-masted schooner built in 1869 by Richard Pickard and John Leonard for the Rolle Canal Company. She was launched without her masts and floated through Bideford Bridge with barely an inch and a half to spare. Her masts were stepped-in at the quayside in Bideford. The yard eventually closed in 1875, some five years after the canal ceased operation.

The first vessel to travel up the new canal was the May, a 70 tonner of Bristol, with a cargo of coals from Newport – a gift from Lord John Rolle to the poor of Torrington to mark the occasion. The May was equipped with "a striking mast in order to pass Bideford Bridge". The cargo was transferred into 4-ton boats or tubs, which were then lifted up the inclined plane to the canal. A string of six tubs were drawn by one horse along the canal to Torrington. Regular traffic was coal and limestone from Wales, and of course clay from Peters Marland, with agricultural produce travelling in the opposite direction. The opening of the Rolle Canal meant that the means of bulk transport were now much closer at hand. The clay could now be taken by pack horses the five or six miles to Torrington, where it was loaded onto barges for transfer to the port of Bideford, from where the cargo would be transferred to sea-going vessels. And so, for the next 45 years, until the Torrington Extension Railway was opened, the Marland clay and bricks were hauled up the narrow, winding roads to the canal at New Manor Mill, and thence conveyed to the river and so on to sea and off to the four

corners of the world. Pack animals gave way to the horse and cart, and the new-fangled traction engine and steam lorry in turn replaced this method in the latter part of the nineteenth century.

In a lease dated 25th September 1860 the operation of the canal was leased by the trustees of the late Lord Rolle to George Braginton – whom we met earlier – for a period of 21 years at an annual rent of £207. The lease, which was effective from 25th October 1859, contained a proviso that if the canal was ever required for the purposes of constructing a railway, then the lease could be terminated by twelve months notice to Mr Braginton. The Railway Company would be liable to pay compensation for loss of trade incurred in the notice period. Such notice was never served, for Braginton's bank failed in 1865 and he was made bankrupt. The canal thus reverted to the Rolle Estate. The Torrington Extension Railway from Bideford to Torrington opened in 1872 and closely followed the bed of the Rolle Canal, which was thus effectively closed down. Whilst the railway did provide a reliable method of transport, it was still some 6 miles from the clay works and the need for a proper integrated transport system was becoming of paramount importance to the Clay Company. In the absence of any action by the LSWR to extend the Torrington line southwards, or the likely early fruition of any of the other proposed routes in the area, the Marland Clay Company had no other course of action but to consider building their own railway to Torrington to enable trans-shipment of their products on to the rapidly expanding national railway network.

NOTICE.

A Meeting of the Parties entitled to Commonable or other Rights over or in Great Torrington Common,

Situate in the Parish of Great Torrington, in the County of Devon, will be held

AT THE TOWN HALL, GREAT TORRINGTON, AFORESAID,

On Tuesday, the 14th day of October inst.,

At Seven o'Clock in the evening,

For the purpose of receiving an application from the Promoters of a Light Railway, for leave to carry their proposed Line through a portion of the said Common adjoining or near the Torrington Railway Station, and appointing a Committee to treat with such Promoters for the compensation to be paid for the same.

Dated this Sixth day of October, 1879.

Signed on behalf of the Promoters,

GEO. DOE,

Solicitor, Great Torrington.

Notice of Meeting re Commons.
The notice advertising the meeting of Commoners and other interested parties to be held in the Town Hall on 14th October 1879 for the purpose of discussing the proposed new light railway.
(The Beaford Archive)

Chapter 3

RAILS TO THE CLAY WORKS

The pressure to solve the transport problem between the clay workings and Torrington eventually became irresistible, and in 1879 an approach was made by Frederick Holwill of the Marland Brick & Clay Company to Mr John Barraclough Fell, who was by this time a well established name as a railway engineer "of great experience and invention", to survey the route for a new railway to connect the clay works at Peters Marland with the LSWR metals at Torrington station.

At first sight it might seem rather strange as to how Fell – a railway engineer of international repute – became involved with surveying and constructing this little, privately-financed line in the depths of North Devon. It appears from published reports that the answer is simplicity itself; Frederick Holwill of the Marland Company made a direct approach to J.B. Fell. Holwill was a man of some standing locally: a former Alderman, a Charity Trustee, and High Bailiff to the County Court. He was listed in Harrod's Directory for 1878 as being "Ship owner, coal, lime, timber, brick & clay merchant. South Street, Torrington and at Marland Brick & Tile Works". Frederick Holwill was clearly a man who kept abreast of developments and it is hard to imagine him not having his finger on the pulse of what was going on in the world. He would have been aware of Fell's work in constructing the Mont Cenis Railway, the Cantazallo Railway in Brazil, and – another clay based line – the

Beam Aqueduct
A lithograph of the Aqueduct that carried the Rolle Canal over the River Torridge, roughly midway along its length. The main Torrington to Bideford road now passes just behind this viewpoint and the aqueduct is now the road access to an adventure holiday centre at Beam House.
(Author's collection)

27

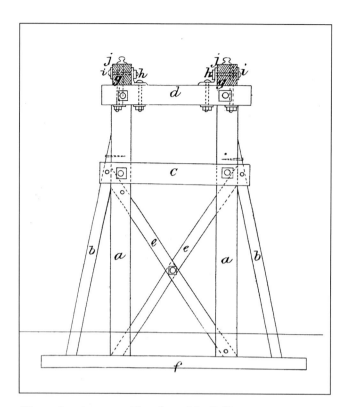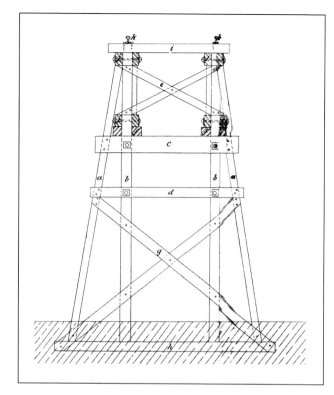

These drawings are taken from J.B. Fell's patents 1638 and 1249 and illustrate the various types of pier and bridge sections on which Fell's ideas were based. It was these that were used throughout the Torrington & Marland line. Note the method of sinking the piers into the ground and lack of foundation. Given the exceptionally high quality of the timber, this did not seem to present a major problem. Left: A section of a bridge pier showing cross bracing and bolt positions. Right: A similar section of a pier for greater height, showing additional bracing.

Pentewan Railway in Cornwall. Although only of 8in gauge, the Parkhouse Mineral Railway near Barrow-in-Furness was probably the first major example of Fell's trestle type of construction and this lead to the pioneering, but experimental, Aldershot Railway for the War Department. Fell's vigour and enthusiasm in publicising his patented narrow gauge railway system would have been well known, if not always appreciated, in railway engineering circles. Holwill would also have been aware of Fell's friendship and working relationship with Thomas Brassey, who had built and operated the North Devon and Bideford Extension Railways. With the Marland Clay Company in such need of improved transport services, these factors must all have contributed to Fred Holwill's conviction that a light railway was the answer to their problems and that John Barraclough Fell was the man to provide it.

The new line being proposed by the Clay Company was a far cry from most of the work that Fell had undertaken in the past, both in terms of complexity and in monetary value, but John Fell must have thought that here, in North Devon, was the opportunity he had long been seeking and hoping for in order to put his ideas into practise on a much larger scale than either the Aldershot or Pentewan railways. Here, with virgin territory at his disposal, he could fully exploit his patented system of construction and produce a line that would

utilise the Fell trestles instead of cuttings and embankments and, in the undulating hinterland of North Devon, leap across river, stream and road on Fell viaducts and bridges. Motive power would of course be in the hands of Fell-designed locomotives. Fell might well have thought that all this might at last convince the War Office to take up his patent system for military use.

So, early in 1879, John Barraclough Fell arrived in Torrington to meet the Marland Company and local officials preparatory to carrying out his survey for a new line of railway. Fell was 64 years of age at this time – a good age in those days – and it is almost certain that his elder son, George Noble Fell, accompanied him from the start to assist in the work. George was 30, about to be married, and a civil engineer like his father. It is likely that he would have been responsible for much of the routine work on his father's behalf. Certainly he was involved in the preparation of the contract specification and drawings and it would seem fairly certain that he was living in Torrington for much of the time. What arrangements were initially made for accommodation is not known, but certainly by the following year if not earlier, once approval had been given for construction, J.B. Fell had taken up residence at Warren House on the edge of the town. This was a large and gracious house overlooking the Torridge and Pencleave Valleys and was well situated for the purposes

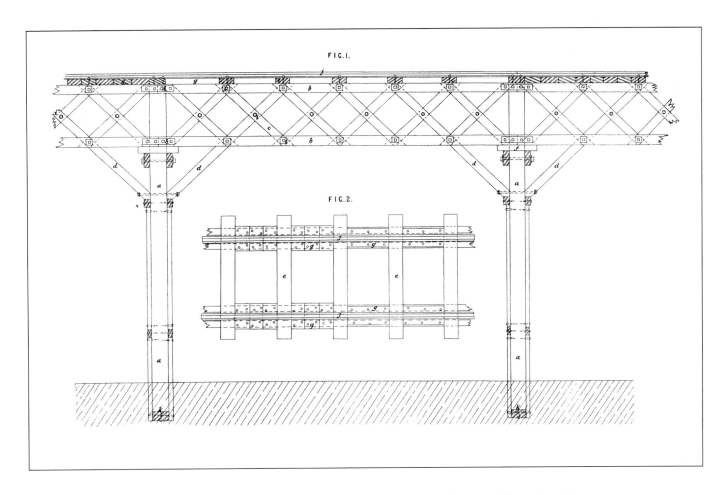

A side view of a standard bridge unit with inset of track layout showing rail and cross tie (sleeper) positions.

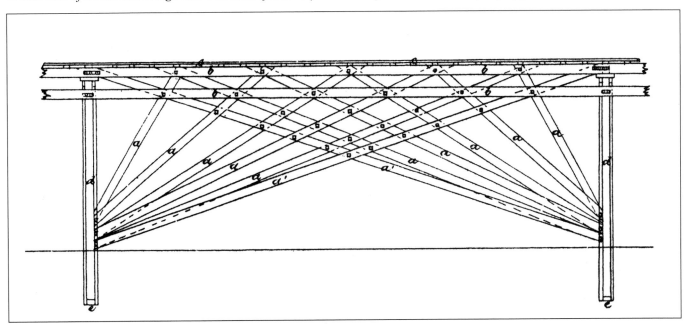

A view of a braced section for use in viaducts. It is from this patent drawing (figure 13 of patent 1638,) that the main section of the Torridge viaduct was built.

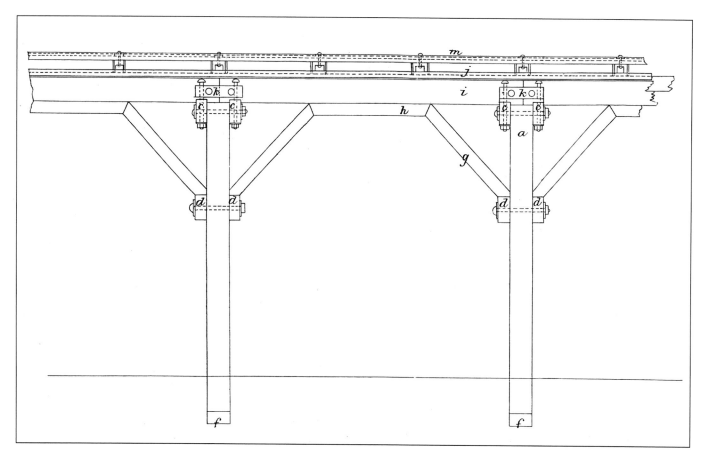

A short span bridge fitted with centre rail.

of its new tenant, being less than half a mile from Torrington station. The house belonged to James Balsden, a local farmer and immediate past Mayor of the Borough, and a man thus well acquainted with Frederick Holwill, who had no doubt made the introductions and arrangements. George Fell, once married, seems to have been living in Northam, not far out of Bideford and only a few miles from Torrington.

Holwill had clearly done the groundwork with the local landowners and the Town Council, but the Fells, father and son, had to discuss their proposals with them as well as survey the route. The small matter of providing a transfer siding and other accommodation in Torrington station goods yard had also to be discussed and agreed with the LSWR. Other considerations were such things as arranging supplies of timber for the bridges and sleepers, and stone for ballast. Whilst the timber for the main structures would have to be imported – not a problem for J.B. Fell, who started out in life as a timber merchant – other timber could be obtained locally, as could the stone from local quarries. And what of the men who would carry out the actual construction work – the navvies and labourers? Were they to be brought in by the Fells or recruited locally? All of these matters and more would occupy father and son over the next few months.

The middle part of 1879 saw the surveys completed and

the route decided, with the requisite plans and drawings prepared and submitted to the Marland Brick & Clay Company for consideration. The original drawing shows two alternative routes near Watergate Bridge, about a mile and a half out of Torrington. The final alignment involved the crossing of a small river and then a road crossing, instead of crossing two roads and keeping to the east of the river and making a crossing later. Apart from a short descent out of Torrington, the line was to climb steadily to a summit at Yarde from where it descended all the way to the clay works.

Terms had then to be agreed with the landowners concerned for the leases on the land required for the line. The Hon Mark Rolle, Lord Clinton, J.C. Moore-Stevens Esq, and J.G. Johnson Esq, seem to have been readily agreeable to provide the land, and the only remaining landowner was the Torrington Commons Conservators, the people of Torrington responsible for the Commons. A meeting was held at Torrington Town Hall on Tuesday, 14th October 1879 of those interested parties and, seeing that the railway would be of benefit to the town, it was agreed to allow part of the Commons land to be used, and a committee was appointed to deal with the matter accordingly. On 27th December 1879 a meeting of the Highway Board in Torrington considered a letter from:

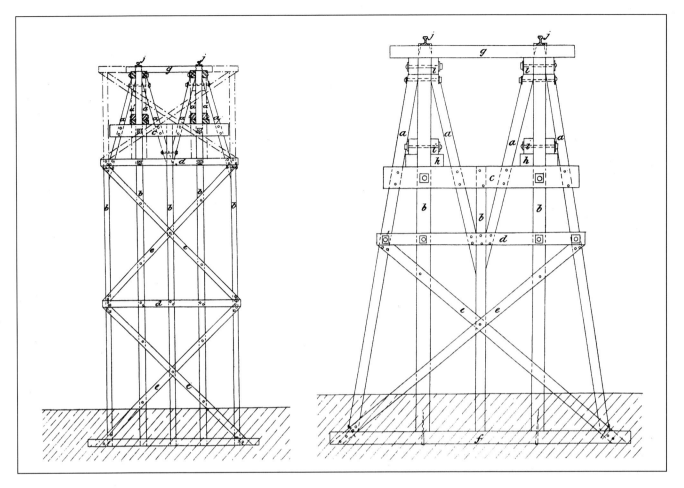

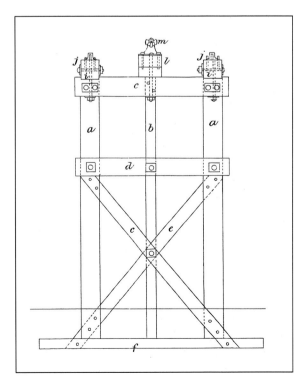

Above left: A section of a bridge pier for use at greater heights and weights than that seen on page 28.

Above right: A section of an alternative type of pier with less cross bracing than the adjoining drawing.

Right: A plain pier for use with low trestle bridges.

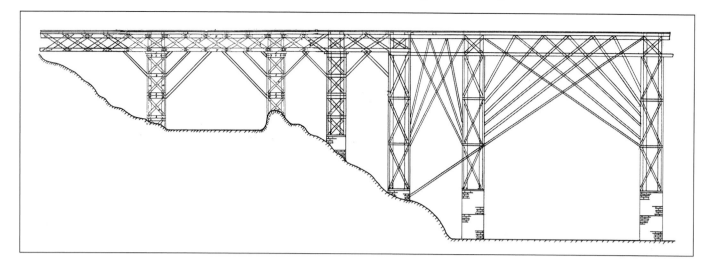

Above and opposite: A plan of the Torridge Viaduct prepared using the drawings in Fells patents and photographs of the actual structure. The actual contract drawing must have looked very similar. (Not to scale.)
(Matthew Cole)

"The Engineer of the proposed Torrington and Marland Railway accompanied by plans and statement showing the proposed crossings of the Highway and Turnpike Road. Resolved that the Board offer no objection to the proposed Railway provided that the Committee appointed by the Board can make satisfactory arrangements for the safety and convenience of the Public."

This decision cleared the way for final surveys and setting out to commence.

In January 1880, a joint meeting was held of the Council and the Trustees of the Town and Alms Lands to consider the passage of the new railway under the main turnpike road just outside the existing Torrington station.

"The Town Clerk produced a plan and statement relative to the proposed Railway from Torrington Station to the Marland Clay works being carried below the Turnpike Road near the Station together with a resolution of the Turnpike Trustees on the subject – Resolved that the Council offer no objection to the proposal provided that it be carried out with the least possible inconvenience to the public."

The stage was now set for the actual work of construction to begin, but before we take a look at how this was carried out, it is pertinent to pause and consider the contractual and design part of the operation and consider how this relates to John Fell's overall plans and aspirations.

In the early days of railway construction, comparatively little of the work to be done was formalised or written down, and individual contractors usually undertook only small parcels of the whole work. The word "contractor" is used carefully, as the contractor could range from an individual foreman or ganger with a group of men under his loose control, to someone like Thomas Brassey or Samuel Morton Peto employing thousands. To start with however, the work would be let by the engineer, or the company, in small parcels: a bridge here, a mile of line there, a very short tunnel somewhere else. The net result could be many individual contracts, often organised verbally with nothing in writing apart from the engineer's drawings. The risk of the failure of one contractor bringing the whole work to a halt was thus minimised.

Contract specifications, agreements and tenders were rare; all three together in one contract was probably unknown. J.U. Rastrick, the engineer to the Kenyon & Leigh Railway in Lancashire claimed, in a report to the Birmingham Committee of the London & Birmingham Railway in 1833, to have drawn up "the first regular specification that was ever made out for the construction of a Railway" which was "the model for almost every work of the kind that has since been set about". His contracts insisted upon the contractor supplying performance guarantees to safeguard the Company's position in the event of a failure by the contractor. A full specification had to be drawn up by the engineer, and the size of each contract determined at the outset. With the protection of formal contracts including specifications and drawings and backed by guarantees, engineers like Locke were able to award much larger contracts to those contractors who had proved themselves on earlier work. Thus began such fruitful and profitable associations as that between Joseph Locke and Thomas Brassey.

The full text of Fell's specification, and the two contracts for the construction of a railway from Torrington to Peters Marland are too long for reproduction here, but we

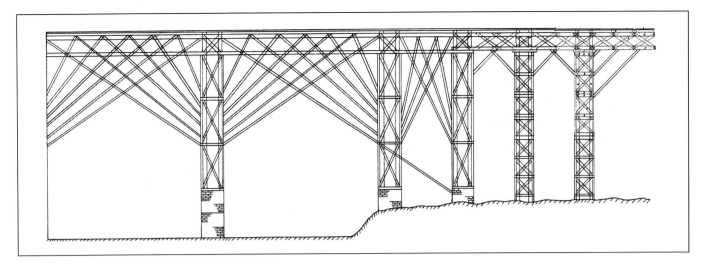

shall need to discuss their content in the text of this consideration. The drawings of the various bridge and viaduct structures referred to in the text of the Specification are still in existence apart, unhappily, from the drawings for the Torridge Viaduct which have apparently deteriorated to such an extent that they are not now available to view or for research purposes. However, this latter point is addressed later.

The Contracts

The Marland Brick & Clay Works Limited appointed J.B. Fell as Engineer (8th June 1880), to superintend and direct; and the Green Odd Railway & General Contracting Company Limited as Contractors (1st May 1880), for the execution of the works "of the Light Railway now in course of construction between the works of the said Company at Peters Marland in the County of Devon and the terminus of the London and South Western Railway at their Station at Torrington in accordance with the Plans, Sections and Specifications already prepared…"

The total contract value was £10,580 and Fell's fee was to be 5% of this plus the sum of £105 in respect of extra surveys and other additional, unspecified, expenses he had incurred. Payment to contractors was often made by way of an issue of shares in the company and the Marland Company was up-to-date with current commercial practise and accordingly, Fell's fee was to be paid largely in shares. Of the total £634 due to him, £500 would be paid as 2 x £250 fully paid up shares in the Company and the rest (£134) in cash. £105 in cash was to be paid on or about 15th June – within about a week of the contract being signed – together with the first £250 share. The balance of the other share and the rest of the cash would follow "when the works have been completed and the Railway is ready to be opened for traffic". As we know, the cost eventually came in at approximately £15,000 but whether John Fell received an extra £221 being 5% on the additional £4,420 is not known. One would

suspect that there would have been some resistance to this by the Marland Board, although it is interesting to note that the share directory for the Marland Company as at 14th March 1885 shows John B. Fell as holding 10 shares and the Green Odd Company holding 3 shares. One would imagine that Fell must have received an extra fee in view of the higher eventual contract price, and additional work must have been carried out on the Railway in the maintenance period and after. It is interesting to contemplate whether his dual role of Engineer to the Marland Company and as major shareholder in the Contracting Company was raised at any time and if so, whether this fact was used in determining any additional fee to him as Engineer.

The Green Odd Company's contract was also based on payment split between cash and shares. The initial contract price of £10,580 was to be divided between an allocation of 6 x £250 shares (£1,500) and £9,080 in cash. 90% of the cost was to be paid upon production of monthly Engineer's certificates, 5% would be paid upon completion of the works and the remaining 5% would be paid after the expiry of the 6 months maintenance period. "Shares to be taken in payment of the Instalment (sic) next preceding the payment of the last Ten (sic) per cent and so as to leave that payment to be made in cash. Provided that the amount of Engineer's Certificates for extra or additional work shall be paid entirely in cash." Clearly the contractor needed cash for the payment of wages and cost of materials, hence the higher cash to share ratio in this case.

The contract had certain provisions built in to protect both the Company and the Contractor and we can see that it contained many of the provisions that a modern contract would incorporate, although perhaps on a smaller scale.

The contract provided for work to start within one month of the date of the contract and allowed seven months for completion. The initial draft only allowed six months but this was amended in the final document. A penalty clause provided for liquidated damages at a daily rate of five pounds (£5) to be paid for each day the contract overran – other than by *force majeur.* The penalty to be paid weekly. There was provision for a corresponding daily rate to be paid to the contractor if the contract was completed early.

The contractor was responsible for making good any damage, etc caused by "accidental causes" or by "Storm Tempest Trespassers or other means" which occurred prior to the issuing of the Engineers Certificate on completion of the whole of the works, and also during the six month maintenance period, other than for damage caused "by Trespassers or from wilful damage" and excluding reasonable wear and tear.

Sunday working was prohibited, unless for safety reasons.

All materials brought on to the premises became the property of the Company, as did plant and machinery until the works were completed.

The Contractor was to keep an Agent or Foreman on the site at all reasonable times, and he was to be considered to be the agent for the Contractor.

The Schedule of Prices was deemed to include all labour, machinery etc and was to be the total to be paid for all the work.

The Company or the Engineer was allowed to modify the work to be done and any adjustments in payment to be made in accordance with the Schedule of Prices, except that the minimum payment should not fall below £10,580.

If the Engineer was not satisfied with the progress of the works he could order additional hands to be employed and if after seven days he was still not satisfied he could use any of the materials and employ additional hands and charge the contractor accordingly.

If monthly payments by the Company fell overdue by more than seven days, the Contractor could suspend work until such payments were received. Compensation would be payable and the contract period was to be extended accordingly.

The contractor *was allowed to use earthworks instead of timber viaducts* (author's italics), except in the Torridge valley, but cuttings or embankments were not to exceed seven or eight feet.

The line of the railway could be deviated by the contractor up to fifty yards in order to save on costs, provided that there was no increase in gradient, nor reduction in curves below a radius of ten chains. The contractor was responsible for any negotiations with landowners.

If the contractor were to fail, then payment would be made to him at a rate of 75% of the value work certified by Engineer's certificate.

The Engineer was to be *the sole judge* (author's italics) of all differences between the parties.

To follow the progress of Fell's designs, and the effect on the construction of the Torrington & Marland Railway, a summary of his patents is shown in Table 3.

The first seven of John Fell's patents relate to his ideas

Patent Number	Date of issue	Nature
227	26th January 1863	Working of engines, etc on steep inclines.
3182	16th December 1863	Railway engines and carriages, etc.
2174	24th August 1866	Locomotive engines and carriages.
766	5th March 1868	Locomotive engines, carriages, etc.
899	24th March 1869	Locomotive engines, railways, etc.
1	2nd January 1871	Locomotive engines.
1246	9th May 1871	Railways.
1014	19th March 1873	Improvements in the construction of light railways. Joint patent with G.N. Fell.
1638	26th April 1879	Improvements in the construction of light railways, and in locomotive engines to be employed thereon.
1249	24th March 1880	Improvements in the construction of railways.
3579	28th July 1882	Improvements in locomotive engines for railways.
6718	7th April 1892	Locomotive engines and permanent way.
762	12th January 1895	Improvements in engines for traction.

Table 3. Patents issued to J.B. Fell

A view from the riverside, looking up at the viaduct from the southern side, with Torrington station lying to the right of this view. (The Beaford Archive)

for very narrow gauge, probably elevated, lines where a centre rail would be used for stability and possibly adhesion and braking as well. It is the next four that have relevance to wider gauges, and to those lines where a centre rail would not necessarily be used; it is these that are of concern to us here. Reference is made to locomotives in some of the patents, but it is with structures with which we are currently interested. The text of the first of these patents, No. 1014 which he took out jointly with his son, starts "Our invention relates to improvements in the construction of light railways of any gauge, but generally of gauges of two feet and upwards, and they are also adapted for railways on which the centre rail system is to be used." Note the use of the expression "light railways" here. The patent continues:

"The object of our invention is economy in the construction, working and maintenance of railways by dispensing wholly or partly with earth works, masonry, and ballast and by using as a substitute for them a structure of wood or iron consisting of supports formed of two upright or inclined pillars or posts, connected together by suitable cross ties strengthened in some cases by external lateral struts and by diagonal braces

fixed between the upright pillars, which latter rest upon a sill or sleeper placed on or sunk under the surface of the ground. For centre rail lines and for broader gauges a third or central post may be used… These forms of structure may be used in combination with the ordinary description of permanent way laid on the surface of the ground on embankments, or in cuttings where it is convenient to use such on any portions of the line."

Patent 1014 thus sets out the basic idea for the Fell "trestle" system, which is intended for railways of 2 feet gauge and above, but interestingly mentions that it is suitable for 4 feet 8½ inch gauge lines. The following patent (1638) is intended to show improvements over its predecessor with more substantial construction. The use of the "Warren" type girder is introduced, and construction of wider spans is envisaged. Use in military field railways is contemplated. Patent 1249 came next and provided for additional support for greater strength. Greater height of structures was allowed for in this development.

The last figure of Patent 1638 is for "a side elevation of a timber structure composed of lattice girders of a form adapted for wider spans than any of those previously described, the lower end of the lattice bars being continued through to the vertical supports on the two sides of the span". In other words, a viaduct such as that over the Torridge. So, whilst we do not have the original drawing of the viaduct it is possible to construct an approximation from this drawing in the patent, and by reference to actual photographs of the viaduct, as shown in the drawing featured earlier.

It is thus possible to link the contract drawings very closely to the corresponding drawings in the patents – although it would be strange indeed if they were not identical, in view of the closeness of the dates, and on this basis, we can see that the Torridge viaduct must have been built to figure 13 of patent 1638 (shown on page 29).

In summary therefore we can equate the various types and size of structure to both contract drawing and patent drawing, as shown in Table 4.

Table 4. *Drawing and patent figure number for bridges*

Bridges	Drawing	Patent	Figure
3ft – 15ft	4, 5, 5A	1638/1249	10/1 and 3
15ft – 30ft	6, 7, 8	1638	7 / 11 and 12
Viaduct	9, 10, 10A	1638	13

The Specification

The specification commences with an explanation of the use of timber instead of earthworks. It goes on to set out the methods to be used where cuttings and embankments are used, and also stipulates the requirement for soiling and grassing of these. The salient points of the specification as regard to conformity with the patents really relate to the viaducts and bridges. These are to be as per the contract drawings depending on their height, and specific and detailed procedures are then given as to sizes of components and methods of fixing. Details of piling in the bed of the Torridge and depth of supports on dry ground are also given. Great emphasis is given to the use of the right drawing for the right conditions – straight or curved sections of track require different support. The Bill of Quantities (Appendix C) sheds more light on the construction as we are given details of amounts of timber required for differing heights and lengths of viaduct and bridge, and also the total lengths of trestlework to be used. On a total line of 6¼ miles there was to be just over 2 miles of viaduct (2 miles 2 chains). Only 6½ furlongs were on the level, and the rest was to be relatively shallow cutting or embankment. The average heights of viaducts range from 5ft to 35ft and are given in 5ft increments; the former make up almost a mile of the line. It is quite clear then from this that Fell's "improved" system was to be used to avoid as much excavation as possible, and that with the use of standardised sections for virtually all eventualities, construction would have been very considerably easier than with conventional methods. The details of the bridge under the Turnpike Road outside Torrington station are given, but alas no details of how this was to be accomplished, so we do not know if it was an excavated tunnel or if a cut and cover

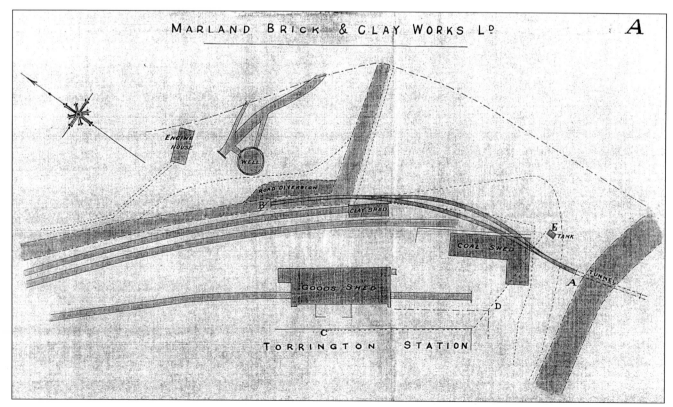

Rails to the Clay Works

The LSWR's plans of the siding at Torrington Station

The first plan (opposite page) for the transfer siding at Torrington station as appended to the formal agreement between the Clay Company and the LSWR. This shows a run-round loop in the station yard and a dead-end siding feeding a clay shed. The practicalities of this arrangement seem doubtful; a view obviously shared by the two parties at the time. (The North Devon Records Office)

Right: The plan of the arrangements as actually made, showing the long siding between the two standard gauge lines, thus facilitating transfer of clay to either line. Although there are two short sidings (or headshunts) shown, which would have accommodated an engine, it appears that the engine based at Torrington spent the night under cover in the short tunnel just past point A on the plan. It is not certain that the siding off the facing point by the first shed was actually laid or used; it is missing on some contemporary maps, but others do show it. This second plan is also of more general interest, as it shows most of the layout of the main part of the station. (Author's collection)

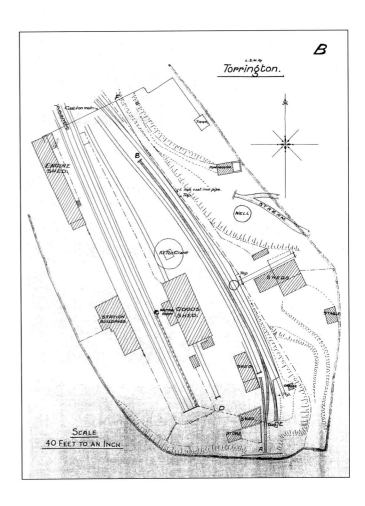

method was used. Rails, of the Vignolles or bridge type, were to be provided by the Marland Company and sleepers were to be oak or Baltic pine and laid 2ft 6in apart. Ballast requirements are laid down, as is the requirement for superelevation on curves.

It is quite obvious that this railway was to be Fell's showpiece, using all his patented methods for construction and locomotion, and there is no doubt that, even at this relatively late stage in his life, he was still hoping for War Office recognition and approval for his ideas, and for government contracts for fixed and prefabricated railways for army use.

The formal commencement of rental agreement with the Rolle Estate (and the other landowners presumably) for the land started on 1st February 1880, and it must have been soon after this the setting-out of the line and preparation on the ground was started, if not already under way by then. The materials required for the contract, and the labour to convert them into a completed railway, were now required. Timber for the main trestles was to be Baltic pine, which obviously had to be imported, and this soon arrived at the site of a steam sawmill set up at Staplevale, close to Torrington railway station. Other timber was obtained locally; surviving correspondence shows much as coming from the Rolle estate.

Ballast was to be obtained from local quarries, of which the area was well supplied, as is seen in surviving letters from the Rolle estate. Labour to construct the railway was under the charge of the Green Odd Company's local agent, Mr R.P. Hirst. Mr Morris is also reported as being one of the contractor's representatives – possibly a Head Office man. Press reports of the day mention the Green Odd Contracting Co as being from Leeds, but a connection with that town has not been traced. Details of the labour force are hard to establish, but the *North Devon Journal* of Thursday, 16th October 1879, in its report on the meeting regarding acquisition of Commons land for the railway, mentions the prospect of "employment for a large number of hands during the winter". It is assumed that Hirst would have brought in a nucleus of experienced men, and recruited the rest locally. No doubt the wages offered would have been quite attractive in a largely rural area, especially if other work was scarce.

The preparatory work proceeded according to plan, and on Wednesday, 26th May 1880, Mrs Mary Elizabeth Fell, wife of George Noble Fell, cut the first sod on Torrington Commons, just outside the existing LSWR railway station. The young couple were possibly out on their first public engagement together, having been married barely two months earlier on the last day of March. (In the light of subsequent

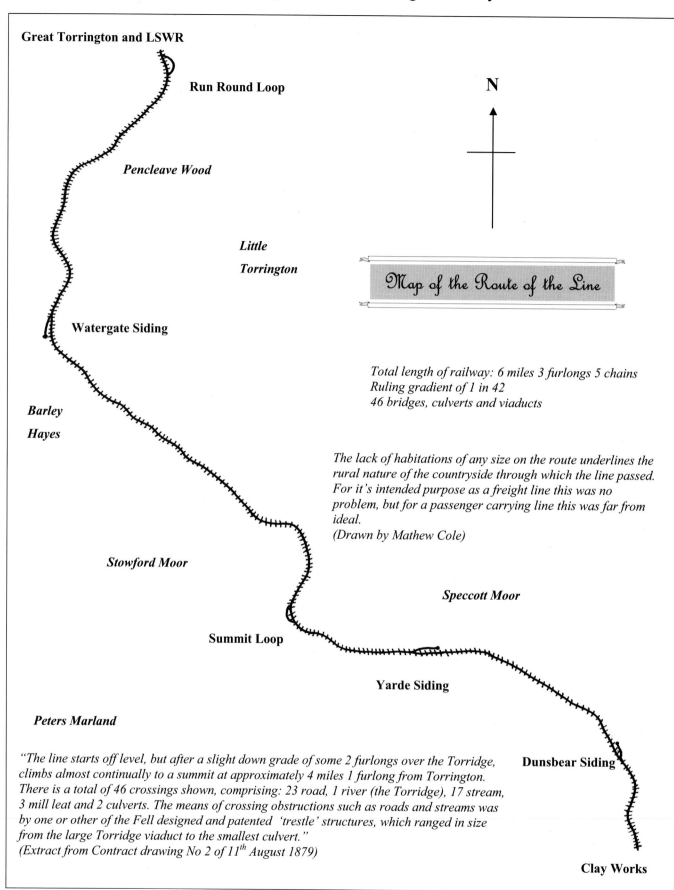

Great Torrington and LSWR

Run Round Loop

Pencleave Wood

Little

Torrington

N

Map of the Route of the Line

Watergate Siding

Total length of railway: 6 miles 3 furlongs 5 chains
Ruling gradient of 1 in 42
46 bridges, culverts and viaducts

Barley

Hayes

The lack of habitations of any size on the route underlines the rural nature of the countryside through which the line passed. For it's intended purpose as a freight line this was no problem, but for a passenger carrying line this was far from ideal.
(Drawn by Mathew Cole)

Stowford Moor

Speccott Moor

Summit Loop

Yarde Siding

Peters Marland

Dunsbear Siding

"The line starts off level, but after a slight down grade of some 2 furlongs over the Torridge, climbs almost continually to a summit at approximately 4 miles 1 furlong from Torrington. There is a total of 46 crossings shown, comprising: 23 road, 1 river (the Torridge), 17 stream, 3 mill leat and 2 culverts. The means of crossing obstructions such as roads and streams was by one or other of the Fell designed and patented 'trestle' structures, which ranged in size from the large Torridge viaduct to the smallest culvert."
(Extract from Contract drawing No 2 of 11th August 1879)

Clay Works

events related in a later chapter, the occasion takes on a degree of poignancy.)

The *North Devon Journal* were clearly geared up for the event, for the following day they carried this brief report, (the preamble has been left in to show the patriotic nature of the local populace):

"Torrington

Monday last being the Queen's birthday, the bells of St Michaels's Church sent forth merry peals at intervals in honour of the occasion.

THE MARLAND RAILWAY. - On Wednesday last, the ceremony of cutting the first sod of the above Railway was performed by Mrs Fell, wife of Mr. Fell jun, Engineer. Several of our townsfolk walked to the spot to witness the ceremony, and a number of gentlemen more or less connected with the scheme were also present. Mrs. Fell performed her part of the ceremony, namely, lifting the sod into the barrow, and wheeling it a little distance, in excellent style, and on her tipping the sod from the barrow the company gave three loud cheers. The party afterwards adjourned to Warren House, where Mr Fell snr, has taken lodgings. Several navvies were

on the spot, which is near the Fir Trees, just opposite Torrington station, and the work of construction is to be proceeded with at once."

The following Thursday, they published a more detailed version of the event, which included a full description of the line, and a list of those present.

Once started work proceeded apace and on 24th and 29th June 1880, the *North Devon Journal* and *Bideford Gazette* respectively both reported:

"THE MARLAND RAILWAY. – The work of constructing the above light railway from our station to the Marland clay pits is now being rapidly pushed on by the contractor. Several men are at work close to the station in preparing for cutting the tunnel, or making an archway under the turnpike road; whilst a large relay of hands are at work throwing up an embankment on the opposite side of the river, near Drummett's Mill, extending it towards the river, so as to meet the bridge to be constructed across the Torridge. A large quantity of timber, planks, &c., has been received and deposited in a field near Staple Vale Farm, close to the

"Mary" runs off the viaduct with a train of empties bound for the works. The railway cottages above the station can be seen in the distance on the left of the picture. (The Beaford Archive)

The Torrington & Marland Light Railway

Left: A good view of the trestle bridge at the end of the viaduct.

Bottom: Looking back along the tracks to the viaduct. The road from the station to Torrington runs up the hill from left to right.

(The Beaford Archive)

Marland Line and Station Hill, Torrington. 148   Dyer, Torrington.

Rails to the Clay Works

A nice view of the Torridge viaduct and the Rolle Road. The river level appears to be low, so this is probably a summertime shot.
(Tom Bartlett Postcard Collection, Berrynarbor, EX34 9SE)

railway station, where it is to be cut by a steam saw and prepared for use in constructing the permanent way of the line. We hear that upwards of a mile of the road near the clay works has already been prepared for the laying of metals, &c. The heaviest work will be near our railway station namely, that of constructing the bridge and the cutting under the road: in the latter case, we believe, it has been considered necessary to make a temporary roadway near the old fir trees, to be used for general traffic until the tunnel (or archway) shall have been completed."

The reference in this article to the steam saw at Staplevale gives us an idea of the considerable activity that must have been going on at that site. As the timberwork for the trestles, bridges, viaducts, etc, was designed to Fell's patents and specification, it is logical to assume that this would be all have been produced at Staplevale for the whole line. A mass-production operation would see timber cut to size for each location and sent out, either ready made in sections, or effectively in kit form, ready for easy assembly and erection on site. Whilst the contractor's men were busy digging and building, discussions were taking place, and letters passing to and fro regarding stone for ballast and

timber amongst other things. A considerable amount of this correspondence was with the Rolle Estate and a number of the letters written from the estate office by Mark Rolle's staff have survived in the estate letter books. From these we see that both John Barraclough Fell and George Noble Fell, as well as Fred Holwill at the Clay Company, were in touch with the estate. July 1880 sees correspondence regarding stone from the estate quarry, the tipping of spoil, meetings regarding felling trees and valuation thereof, and the acquisition of addition land for the cutting at Langtree Week. The correspondence starts with a letter dated 17th July 1880 to:

"Mr F Holwill, Torrington
Dear Sir,
Before Mr Lipscomb gives the contractor for the Clay Moor Light Railway permission to obtain stone from the Watergate Quarry he would like to know about what number of loads would be required – the price we should charge for the stone would be 2d per load. Yours faithfully,
A L J Morley"

A reply was clearly forthcoming for on 21st July 1880, Morley responded with:

The Torrington & Marland Light Railway

*A similar view to that on the previous page, but showing more of the approach trestles at the end of the viaduct.
(The National Railway Museum)*

"You can take the 500 loads of stone which the Marland Brick & Clay Company may require from the Watergate Quarry, Langtree but the quarry must be worked subject to my approval – the price will be 2d per load – no more surface is to be broken than what is actually necessary."

On 22nd July, George Fell was the recipient of a letter from Mr Morley:

"Dear Sir,
Mr Lipscomb has no objection to the Contractor for the Clay Moor Light Railway depositing soil from the cutting near Torrington Railway Station on the Staple Vale Willow bed provided we obtain the consent of the Tenant, Mr Pow and agree to compensate him for any surface damage that may be committed. I have today written to Mr Pow and said that I understand he has no objection to the above…"

Morley's letter to Mr Pow runs as follows:

"Mr Fell the Engineer to the Clay Moor Light Railway has been to this office and asked whether there is any objection to the soil, which is being removed from the cutting adjoining the Torrington Railway Station, being deposited on the Willow Bed at Staple Vale which is in your occupancy.
I have replied that Mr Lipscomb on behalf of Mr Rolle, has no objection to their doing so, provided they obtain your consent and agree to pay you for any surface damage which may be caused. Please reply to this letter.
Yours faithfully, A L J Morley"

In August it was J.B. Fell who was the recipient of a letter, for on the 7th, Morley wrote to him regarding timber:

"Dear Sir,
Mr Lipscomb would be glad if you could fix a day for Mr Rolle's Forester to meet the Contractor for the Clay Moor Light Railway for the purpose of making arrangements for the felling and valuing of the timber which will have to be cleared away in the woods through which the line passes – the Forester's address is – Mr James Barrie, St. Giles, Torrington.
Yours faithfully,
A L J Morley"

A further letter on the 12th followed this; clearly in response to J.B. Fell's reply to the last letter:

A good view of the viaduct, the old Rothern road bridge, and the station.
(Tom Bartlett Postcard Collection, Berrynarbor, EX34 9SE)

"Dear Sir,
Thank you for your letter of yesterday's date. I think Mr Lipscomb will have no objection to the arrangements you propose as to the valuing of timber which will have to be cleared away.
I saw Mr Rolle this morning and he wished me to say that he would be glad if you spare the Scotch Fir tree near to the Torrington Railway Station.
Yours faithfully,
A L J Morley"

(Author's note: There is still one lone fir tree on the bank above the station. From its size it could be up to 200 years old, and thus could be the one in question)

By 17th September, Mr Lipscomb was writing to Holwill about both building stone and ballast under the heading:

"Clay Railway – Langtree Week Quarry.
I have now heard from Mr Bazeley. He writes under yesterday's date as follows: 'I should not wish to prevent the Marland Company from taking stones from my Quarry if it is a convenience to them, but I think it should be understood that they fill in the Quarry when they have finished and that

they pay me for any surface damage done to the land and take every precaution to prevent my cattle from straying. I will leave the question of damage to Mr Cooper their Secretary. Yours faithfully E.A. Bazeley.'
If the terms of the above letter are agreed to and if you will give a letter to that effect I am quite willing on behalf of Mr Rolle that the Marland Company should use the Quarry paying the Royalty of 4d per yard for Building Stone and 2d for Ballasting.
Yours truly,
R W Lipscomb"

It seems that this was a matter that needed a site meeting to discuss further, for on 13th October 1880, Morley writes to Fred Holwill:

"If all goes well I will meet Mr Hill at the Langtree Week cutting next Friday at about 3.30 in the afternoon, and will then see as to the quantity of extra land the Marland Company require."

From this meeting it would appear that George Fell drew up a formal plan for the additional extraction for on 22nd October Mr Lipscomb wrote:

An interesting view of the viaduct from the Rothern Bridge.
(Tom Bartlett Postcard Collection, Berrynarbor, EX34 9SE)

A view of the Torridge viaduct, showing handrails in position.
(Keith Pearson)

Rails to the Clay Works

"G N Fell, Esq. C.E.

Dear Sir,

I was sorry to be too busy (racing against time to get an important letter to Mr Rolle finished before North Post close) [see separate note regarding postal services and local advert] to see you this morning. I have considered the Plan which you have submitted of the enclosures No's. 1309 & 1329 and I agree to the Marland Clay Co: making the excavations thereon shewn and to the proposal to win 500 and 1000 yards of metal from the sites coloured red on the former and 3000 from the site coloured red on the latter @ 3d. per yard. The question of levelling or scarping the excavation can remain open until the excavations are completed: but I may add, that if matters are so arranged that the eye sores which the excavations will create can be and are softened and planted I shall be glad to ask Mr Rolle to make some abatement in the Royalty of 3d. per cubic yard.

Yours faithfully, R H Lipscomb"

Meanwhile, construction work continued with work proceeding well, when the project's only known accident occurred on 23rd October, as reported in the *North Devon Journal* the following Thursday, 28th October 1880:

"TORRINGTON.

Accident – On Saturday last a number of men employed on the light railway were returning from their work on a trolley, when one of them, namely John Newcombe, who was riding in front and propelling the trolley, fell off and was run over. One of his legs was broken and a finger or thumb much injured. The unfortunate man, was removed to his home, where his sufferings were relieved by medical aid."

By the beginning of December work was apparently well advanced for the *North Devon Journal* of 2nd December 1880 reported:

"TORRINGTON.

THE MARLAND RAILWAY – The works connected with the construction of the above Railway are being pushed forward very rapidly. The tunnel, close by the South Western Railway Station, is finished and the wooden bridge across the river Torridge and through the marshes on the opposite side is so far advanced as to enable the contractors to pass and repass thereon with the new engine and trucks, the use of which on various parts of the line was much needed for the transit of debris for ballast, &c., on the permanent way. Many persons have been attracted to witness the engine passing over the bridge during the last few days, and the novelty adds a new feature to the view from the top of the hill which is very striking. Various opinions have been expressed with respect to the stability of the bridge and wood network with which it is connected, but of course the engineers must be allowed to be the best judges as to what is required for the traffic which will be made over this part of the work."

The work was pushed on throughout that month and by Christmas the main work was virtually complete. As had been previously arranged, the first revenue earning train made the journey from Peters Marland to Torrington on New Year's Day – a Saturday. The *North Devon Journal* of Thursday, 6th January 1881 carried the announcement:

"TORRINGTON.

OPENING OF THE TORRINGTON AND MARLAND LIGHT RAILWAY.

The first train of bricks and clay passed over this railway from the Marland Company's Works to the South Western Company's station at Torrington, on New Year's Day. This date had been fixed with the contractors for the opening of the railway, and it has been punctually observed, the time occupied in the construction of this railway of 6¼ miles in length, having been exactly seven months.

The bells of St. Michael's church sent forth merry peals at intervals during Friday evening, and continued up to about 1 a.m. on Saturday."

(The latter presumably for New Year, rather than the railway!)

The *Bideford Gazette* also carried the same announcement. However, the day set for the official opening – Wednesday 19th January 1881 – fell in the midst of a period of extremely bad weather, and the event had to be postponed at the last minute as we can see from an article in the *Bideford Gazette* on Tuesday, 25th January 1881:

"TORRINGTON.

This town was visited on Tuesday with a severe snowstorm, which commenced at an early hour in the morning. A strong wind blowing caused the snow to drift so that in some places great difficulty was experienced in travelling. The frost during the last few days has been (the worst) known for many years past.

On Wednesday was the day fixed for the opening of the Torrington and Marland Light Railway, but in the course of the morning we received a communication from the engineer, in which he stated that it was impossible to proceed with the arrangements which were proposed to be carried out on account of the severe snowstorm which had been experienced."

This article refers to the delay in the official opening of the Torrington & Marland as being due to a "severe snowstorm" and initially that statement was taken at face value and nothing more. However, upon studying other newspapers of the period, and additional sources, for further information on the railway, it soon became apparent that this was not just a short localised spell of bad weather, but something much more serious and far-reaching. Appearing under the heading "Great Frost and Snowstorm", The *Devon Weekly Times* of Friday, 21st January reported that: "January

"Mary" poses with an Officers Special on one of the viaducts. It is believed that this scene dates back to January or February 1881 when the line was just opening. The snow ties in with the bad weather at the time, as detailed in the text. It is just possible to discern that the locomotive is in original condition, with virtually no cab protection at all.
(Keith Pearson)

1881 will be memorable for the severest weather known during the past 40 or 50 years". The paper had several pages devoted to the bad weather, with such headlines as "Terrific Gale and Snowstorm", "Immense destruction of property", "The Storm in the West", and "Snowed up on the Great Western". Under the penultimate of these headings were two full columns sub-headed "The Mails and the Railways", part of which read:

"During yesterday (Thursday) at Torrington the usual traffic between the town and station was entirely stopped, the road being quite impassable on account of the snow which has fallen almost continuously since Monday evening. The train due at Torrington on Tuesday evening at 8.55 did not reach there until yesterday (Thursday) morning. Business almost entirely suspended, schools closed… In the streets of Barnstaple, the snow has drifted in some places to a depth of five or six feet, thoroughly blocking all traffic, and almost all the shops throughout the town are closed. Railway communication with Ilfracombe is stopped… In Bideford the snow storm continued without cessation till yesterday afternoon, the fall averaging an extra nine inches. Last

evening there was every indication of a further fall. Traffic is suspended and business at a standstill. The last train, due at 8.45pm on Tuesday, reached Bideford at 5.20 yesterday morning."

The following Friday, the paper gave even more details of the continuing arctic weather: "The Great Snowstorm", "Further Blocking of Roads and Railways", and "Fatal Shipwrecks – Deaths from Exposure". The whole country was gripped by the icy conditions, and gales were wreaking havoc off the coasts with many vessels, and lives, lost.

Fortunately the weather abated somewhat over the following week and it was then possible for J.B. Fell to run his inaugural train to publicise the completion of his latest venture. This was clearly intended to be an event of note to gain maximum publicity for the Fells and it took place on Saturday, 5th February 1881, detailed accounts of which were published in the newspapers of the day.

The *North Devon Journal* published a full account of the events in its issue of Thursday 10th February 1881. This gave an account of the route of the line, together with details of the costs and equipment provided, and a description of the run to

Rails to the Clay Works

Peters Marland. After a trip round the works, the party returned to Torrington and adjourned to the Globe Hotel for "a most excellent dinner"! Many speeches were made, and bonhomie and self-congratulation flowed as freely as the wine. (The article includes a list of the guests on the run, which is included in Appendix A.)

Two days earlier, the *Bideford Gazette* had published its version of the opening run, and their reporter seemed much more impressed than his colleague of the Journal. Part of his report reads:

"At 12 o'clock precisely the whistle blew, and the small party were taken at once gently through a short tunnel, some of them raising a faint cheer. On emerging, however, and getting on to the slender-looking bridge, right above the River Torridge, and from thence on to a timber viaduct, 266 yards in length, and forty feet in height, the feeling of jollity suddenly changed to one of wonder and tremulation – wonder that engineering skill could devise so light a structure combined with safety, and tremulation lest the one thought uppermost in the minds of all should be realised. A looker-on from the common above afterwards informed us that the movement of the train across the viaduct as he looked down upon it presented the appearance of a party of children being conveyed across a toy bridge in perambulators. Even the lazy cattle which had been before quietly grazing in the meadow by the river were startled at this new intrusion upon their quietude, and went frisking along in all sorts of attitudes to seek shelter in the hedge beyond. As however, steam was put on, and we rattled along on what was, comparatively speaking, terra firma, round the thickly wooded slopes of Penclive (sic) Valley, reassurance returned, only to leave us again on finding ourselves on a viaduct crossing a narrow gorge, diving a most picturesque and well studded wood. In fact the scenery through which the lines passes from beginning to end is of such character as can rarely be seen from any railway in England. Over viaducts (ten in number) with perfectly upright supports, through the centre of woods, up steep gradients, over boggy moors, then falling a gradient of one in thirty, all the while making some pretty sharp curves, and all of this on a line not 6½ miles in length is a kind of travelling such as Devonshire people are unaccustomed to in their county. It was possibly this fact that struck terror to the hearts of some of this more innocent and less experienced of the party, but by-and-bye noticing that Mr. Fell himself was at the front, and that the engine was under the complete control of the driver, noticing also that on each viaduct there was a substantial guard rail, and then recollecting, too, that Mont Cenis had been conquered by this same skilful engineer with his light railway, all qualms died away, and the return journey found us devoting more attention to the scenery above and below than to the distance we were from mother earth, and discussing the possibilities of extending this most useful piece of railway on to Hatherleigh, and from there to Sampford Courtenay, there joining the Okehampton line… The first experience of travelling over a light railway may be unpleasant, but everyone saw that the element of complete safety was combined with the lightness and the cheapness of a railway of this kind."

The remarks of the newspaper reporters and the comments made by J.B. Fell in his address are quite interesting and bear some closer scrutiny. The newspaper ventures the hope that the new line could be extended to Hatherleigh and on to Sampford Courtenay on the Exeter–Plymouth line. This, they suggest, could open up the line for through passenger as well as freight traffic. This is indeed precisely what should have happened, as we shall see in a later chapter. How this would have fared is a very interesting question; not from the point of view of traffic, which would probably have been reasonably good, but as to how long it would have been that the "break of gauge" problem would have been tolerated until conversion to standard gauge was contemplated. Whilst admitting that this was a consideration, J.B. Fell dismisses it as having more importance attached to it than it warranted! It also promulgates the idea of similar connections in the future for Bideford–Westward Ho! and Barnstaple–Lynton. (It is pleasing that these were both realised; but badly planned in the first instance and short-lived in both cases. However, at the time of writing, the Lynton and Barnstaple is rising from its long slumber.) The reporter seems in no doubt as to the benefits of "Mr Fell's improved system" – a triumph for Fell's public relations and marketing skills!

Fell himself speaks of an original idea for the Torrington & Marland of a "single" line and it is probable that he is referring here to the idea of using his monorail system. It seems as though this is what Fred Holwill and the Marland Company had in mind at the outset and it was only once they got into discussions with Fell that the use of a conventional line of narrow gauge was decided upon. In view of his later comments regarding Board of Trade inspection, it would seems that Fell certainly had in mind the possibility of extending the line or was still seriously seeing the Torrington & Marland as a way of convincing the War Office of his ideas and patents (or both). Finally, when questioned about the wisdom of using timber for the bridges and viaducts, Fell responds with a clearly previously considered costing on the use of iron and quotes an additional cost of £2,000 for the whole line. He also throws in the idea of using oak instead of pine. No doubt this would also have required an increased capital outlay, but it would be unlikely that the Marland Company were looking as far ahead as either Fell or the reporter from the *North Devon Journal*.

"Mary" – now with cab fitted – is seen again at a later date with a load of clay bound for Torrington.
(Keith Pearson)

INFORMATION OF PUBLIC MEN AND INSTITUTIONS
CONNECTED WITH THE TOWN AND COUNTY.

POST OFFICE AND POSTAL TELEGRAPH OFFICE, FORE STREET.
HENRY FOWLER, POSTMASTER.

ARRIVALS.

LINES OF ROAD AND CHIEF PLACES FROM WHICH MAILS ARE RECEIVED.	ARRIVE AT	DELIVERED AT
London and all parts	7 15 a.m.	8 0 a.m.
North Mail	2 0 p.m.	2 15 p.m.

DISPATCH.

LINES OF ROAD AND CHIEF PLACES OF DESTINATION.	BOX CLOSES AT	MAIL DISPATCHED AT
North Mail	12 50 p.m.	1 0 p.m.
London and all parts	6 10 p.m.	6 20 p.m.

On Sunday there is only one delivery, at 8.0 a.m.; and one dispatch, at 6.20 p.m.
WALL LETTER BOX, Mill street, cleared at 5.15 p.m.
Money Orders granted and paid, and Savings Bank and Annuity business transacted from 9.0 a.m. until 5.0 p.m.; on Saturdays until 8.0 p.m.

Postal Service

As far as the town of Torrington was concerned, postal collections and deliveries were divided between the North, and London and everywhere else! The advertisement shown here – taken from Morris's Directory of 1870 – shows this split and gives the respective collection and delivery times. The reference in Mr R.H. Lipscombe's letter to George Fell (page 45) dated 22nd October 1880 to "North Post close" clearly refers to him hurrying to catch the post at Torrington Post Office at 12.50 pm.

Chapter 4

LOCOMOTIVES and ROLLING STOCK

During his career, John Barraclough Fell had established relationships with some of the leading locomotive builders of the day; in particular with Manning Wardle who provided the motive power for the Aldershot, Cantazallo and Pentewan lines. In view of his early activities with the Mont Cenis and Parkhouse lines, and later with the Rimutaka line, it is certain that he would have been in touch with most of the other companies as well at one time or another.

As Fell's ideas for his system of railways developed, so did those for the locomotives that would operate them. It is pertinent here to consider this development in a little more detail, and first take a look at how his ideas were demonstrated in his various patents.

The summary of Fell's patents was reproduced on page 34, and in simplistic terms it may be said that these reflect the changes and developments of Fell's ideas over the years; his early work on monorails and very narrow gauge centre rail lines moves on to wider gauge with centre rails. The centre rail is then dropped and the more conventional narrow gauge concept with long wheelbase locomotives takes over. That is not to say that Fell abandoned any of his ideas; just that as opportunities presented themselves, he seemed to devote his energies to developing his ideas on to their next stage to meet the needs of the moment.

We can place the patents into groups; the first five patents (227, 3182, 2174, 766 and 899) and the last (762) deal with the centre rail issue, with 766 solely relating to monorails. Numbers 1 and 1246 are concerned with narrow gauge lines with a centre rail, and 6718 was not actually registered. This leaves numbers 1014, 1638, 1249 and 3579 concerned with narrow gauge, non-centre rail matters. As 1014 and 1249 deal only with the trestles for railway construction, it is numbers 1638 and 3579 which are of interest to the locomotive side of our story.

Patent number 1638 of 26th April 1879 is largely concerned with the timber trestles for the railway itself, but the latter part deals with locomotive engines and states:

"For working upon railways constructed as above described a special form of engine is or may be used, the weight of which is distributed as equally as may be over from three to six pairs of carrying wheels, the leading wheels being placed in front of the smoke box, the trailing wheels behind the fire box, and the one or more intermediate pairs of wheels being placed between the fire box and the cylinders. By this arrangement the size and power of the engine can be increased without requiring a corresponding increase in the strength, weight and cost of the structure. By the cylinders being carried between the two pairs of wheels there is less lateral oscillation, and by the fire box being placed between two other pairs of wheels a larger fire box can be obtained than if it were limited to the space between the wheels on the same axle. For passing round sharp curves the leading and trailing wheels of the engine are or may be furnished with radial axles"

This section continues by describing, with drawings, three methods of coupling the drive between two engines permanently coupled together.

Patent number 3579 of 28th July 1882 purely relates to locomotive engines for use on light railways. The first object of the patent is to provide "simple flexible engines to work on curves of short radius, of adequate power, with the weight distributed over greater length of rails" by means of an articulated drive between engine and tender. The second part of the patent is in respect of centre-rail locomotives with horizontally mounted drive wheels.

The Fell locomotives built before the construction of the Marland line was commenced followed the themes developed

A woodcut of "Tudor" (or "Kent"), the Bagnall 0-4-0 inverted saddle tank hired by the railway for a few months. The history of the engine is unclear, as is its eventual fate. (T.D. Allan Civil)

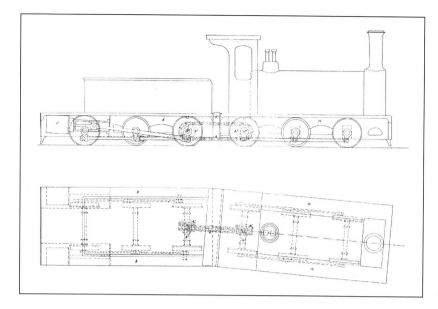

A fascinating "what might have been". Fell's Patent No 3579 of 28th July 1882 with a geared chain drive and universal joints. The position of the cylinders seemingly just on the tender will be noted. Such design was what was later referred to as a "Mallet" type and found favour both in America and more specifically on lightly laid lines on the South American continent.

The lower drawing, from the same patent, refers to a "two-cylinder centre rail Locomotive, the transmission of the motion from the gripping to the carrying wheels or vice versa by means of a supplementary crank shaft or axle and connected parts substantially as hereinbefore described and illustrated by figs 11 and 12 of the drawings".

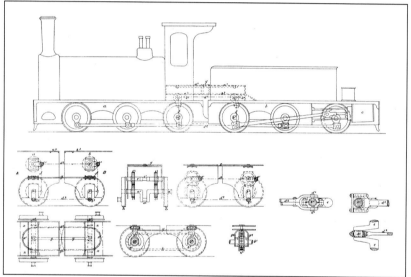

Opposite page: Black Hawthorn 0-6-0 ST "Mary" stands outside the shed at Marland, a whisper of steam confirming that she is awaiting a turn of duty. The enclosed cab was not original and was fitted later.

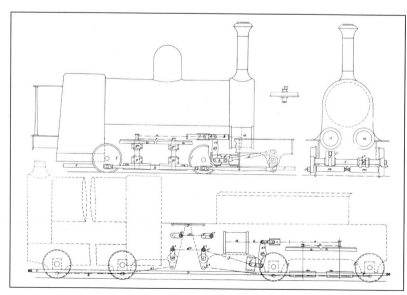

Locomotives and Rolling Stock

in the patents. As Table 5 (which includes the Marland locomotives) shows, it can be seen that each follows the particular patent idea for the prevailing circumstances of its operating location. We can see from these that Fell's main concern is to provide maximum power with minimum axle loading and a low centre of gravity. This principle ensures the maximum benefit in the use of timber trestles for carrying

the railway. Patent 3579 develops the earlier patent 1638 by elongating the powered wheelbase by carrying the final drive to still more axles through articulation in some form. So we can now understand that Fell's ideas have developed from the initial very narrow gauge concept with centre guide rails, which included a monorail system with the option of using two closely spaced rails. He has progressed by widening the

Table 5. Locomotives built for J.B. Fell's railways

Date	Railway	Type	Gauge	Builder	Rail type
1863	Mont Cenis	0-4-0T	3ft 7 5/16 n	Brassey	A
		0-4-0T	1.1m	J. Cross	A
1868	Parkhouse	Cable hauled	8in		B/C
1872	Aldershot	0-6-0 "Ariel"	1ft 6in	Manning Wardle	C
1872	Cantazallo	0-4-0	3ft 7 5/16in (1.1m)	Manning Wardle	A
1873	Pentewan	0-6-0	2ft 6in	Manning Wardle	D
1878	Rimutaka	0-4-2T	3ft 6in	Avonside	A
		0-4-2T	3ft 6in	Neilson	A
1880	Torrington & Marland	0-6-0ST	3ft	Black Hawthorn	D
		0-6-0T	3ft	W G Bagnall	D
		0-4-0T	3ft	Stephen Lewin	D
		0-4-0T "Coffeepot"	3ft	Head Wrightson?	D
		0-6-0ST	3ft	Avonside	D

Key to rail types: *A: Centre rail*
B: Monorail
C: Twin rail with horizontal guide wheels
D: Ordinary narrow gauge

Opposite page and above: W.G. Bagnall 0-6-0T "Marland" is seen at the works, about to leave for Torrington with a train of loaded clay wagons. Believed to have been photographed circa 1913. The centre coupling and side chains can be seen.
(Frank Jones and Roger Carpenter)

gauge to the extent that the centre rail can be dispensed with as an aid to stability, apart from where needed to provide additional adhesive or braking power on the steeper inclines as in Mont Cenis and Rimutaka, and latterly by George Fell in the Isle of Man. The low-slung outline of the earlier style of locomotives, designed to keep a low centre of gravity, gives way to the more conventional type of design, albeit with a longish wheelbase and low axle loading to spread the weight over the timber trestles

The Contract Specification Requirements

The Bill of Quantities in the contract provides, somewhat starkly, for "1 locomotive engine @ £850.0.0d." The main body of the specification stipulates that the timber for the trestles and viaducts shall be "sufficiently strong to carry a six-wheel engine of 6 tons weight the axles being 5 feet apart. The axles of the wagons being placed at the same distances and carrying the same loads as the engine axles." No doubt being on good terms with the locomotive builders Black, Hawthorn & Co, Fell had obviously participated in detailed discussions with them about his requirements for the line, for on 16th June 1880, he sent them the following telegram, which must have been by way of confirmation of the order:

" Marland & Torrington Railway Company, Torrington.
One 7½ inch cylr six wheels coupled 3ft gauge locomotive tank engine as per specification and contract. No name or number. To be delivered in three months without fail.
To be a thoroughly first class job, well finished, to pass Government inspection.
J.B. Fell."

"Peter" is seen here with a group of admirers. (Frank Jones)

The comment regarding Government inspection is interesting, as we know that no inspection was required for the Torrington & Marland, it being a private line. However if we go back to Fell's work on the use of his patents for military railways then perhaps we can begin to see the reason for his choice of words in the telegram. Fell was still keen to convince the War Office that they should back his ideas, and it is reasonable to assume that he saw the Marland line as another instrument he could use to win their support, even thought it was a much wider gauge than the Parkhouse or Aldershot lines. The railway itself would be a tremendous illustration of his ideas in practice, and the presence of a top rate locomotive was also of the greatest importance. It will be seen later that Fell indeed was able to demonstrate the Marland line to the War Office, but with little apparent result.

John Fell's telegram clearly stipulates a delivery date of mid-September 1880 for the locomotive, which would be called "Mary", although it appears that she did not arrive until early December, in time to assist in the final construction of the line. It would seem that "Mary" had to do all the work on the railway herself for the first couple of years, for she was alone until March 1883, when the hired Bagnall 0-4-0 inverted saddle tank locomotive "Tudor" arrived. "Tudor" was hired in at a quarterly rental of £55 with a purchase option of £70. It appears that this locomotive was originally named "Kent", and was not delivered to its original customer but retained by Bagnalls until hired to the Clay Company. The hire contract was for an 18 month period, although it would seem that she only stayed in Devon until December 1883 when the big Bagnall 0-6-0T "Marland" arrived. "Tudor" (or "Kent") went off to reservoir contracts in Lancashire and was last heard of in that area in 1888.

There is no evidence of any problems occurring with "Mary" or her builders, Black Hawthorn & Co, but it was to Bagnall's in Stafford that the order for the next locomotive was given. Possibly experience with "Tudor" had been favourable enough to make Bagnall's the most likely option. "Marland" was ordered in August 1883 and work started on her immediately. She was completed and delivered in December at a cost of £476.5.6d. Invoiced out at £565.0.0d (Net) she produced Bagnalls a useful mark-up of nearly 19%! Bagnall's records show her listed as having spares ordered on 9th July 1894 (order number 383) and 18th August 1897 (order number 435), and on 11th November 1901 it is recorded that a boilermaker from Avonside was on site working on her.

An article in *The Locomotive* of 15th July 1913 mentions "Mary" and "Marland" as both having cylinders of 10in x 12in. J.B. Fell's telegram clearly states 7½in diameter cylinders, so we can assume that these were the correct figures. The same article also states that "Mary" had 1ft 8in

Above and below: The little Stephen Lewin 0-4-0T "Peter" stands by the coal stack. Coaling would not have taken long! The deposits of white clay are obvious on the footplate and the locomotive wheels. (LCGB Ken Nunn Collection)

An official works view of "Avonside" prior to delivery to the Marland Company. (Frank Jones)

wheels with "Marland" having wheels one inch larger. Whether this is correct is difficult to establish, but if measurements were taken at the time, such matters as tyre wear could have accounted for the difference.

It is not clear when the Lewin locomotive "Peter" and the vertical boilered "Coffeepot" came to Peters Marland, but it is safe to assume that they were both in use by 1892 (the approximate date of a prospectus issued by the Company, referred to later) and probably much earlier than that. M.J. Messenger, in his book *North Devon Clay*, suggests no earlier than 1884 for "Peter" and it would seem logical to suggest that both were present by the second half of the 1880s. The rather mysterious vertical boilered "Coffeepot" was probably acquired before "Peter" and worked the clay fields for a while until the Lewin engine arrived on the scene to assist. The growth in traffic over the first few years of the line would warrant a fairly early investment in additional motive power and the two 0-6-0 tanks would have been used on the "main line" between the works and Torrington, leaving the two smaller 0-4-0 tanks to run around the clay fields and marshal trains for onward despatch out of the works.

By the time of the visit of the correspondent of *The Locomotive* in July 1913, there were five locomotives at work. "Mary", "Marland", "Peter", "Avonside" and "Jersey I" were all reported as being present, the mysterious "Coffeepot" having been scrapped about 1908. The same correspondent also reports that all the locomotives were painted a plain dark green with no lining or numbers. They were fitted with centre buffers and side coupling chains. The official works photograph of "Avonside" shows that loco carried a chopper type centre buffer/coupling so this must have been modified for use on the Torrington & Marland.

The three Fletcher Jennings locomotives had been used for work on the harbour breakwater at St Helier and were acquired from the Jersey Harbour Committee in 1908. They had been standing in the open for a few years and it seems that initially only "Jersey I" was fit for work and entered service in 1910, but only after some cannibalisation from the other two engines had taken place. In its original form as a saddle tank engine it was too heavy for the light 30lb rail used on the line, and was rebuilt in 1910, effectively as an 0-4-0 tender engine, with the saddle tank mounted on a wagon towed behind. The other two were however refurbished and also started work in 1914 ("Merton") and 1915 ("Jersey II"). That the original saddle tanks were used as the tender is certain for "Jersey I", and it is possible that the original tanks

Opposite page top and bottom: The first of the Fletcher Jennings 0-4-0 locomotives, "Jersey I"; originally a saddle tank engine, but now carrying its tanks on a flat wagon as a tender. (LCGB Ken Nunn Collection)

"Jersey II" (or possibly "Jersey III") is seen here at Marland on 15th August 1935. (Roger Kidner)

Opposite page top: "Jersey I" sits on the quayside at St Helier on the island of Jersey before shipment to Devon. Note the saddle tanks, later removed to be used as a tender tank. (Frank Jones)

Opposite page bottom: "Jersey I" is seen outside the Marland shed. (LCGB Ken Nunn Collection)

Table 6. *The Torrington & Marland Light Railway 3ft steam locomotives*						
Stock	**Name**	**Type**	**Builder**	**Works number**	**Build date**	**In Use**
1	Mary	0-6-0ST	Black Hawthorn	576	1880	1880-1925
	Tudor/Kent	0-4-0Inv.ST	W G Bagnall	265	1879	1883-1883
2	Marland	0-6-0T	W G Bagnall	566	1883	1883-1925
3	Peter	0-4-0T	Stephen Lewin		1871?	
	"Coffeepot"	0-4-0T	Head Wrightson?		?	18??-1908
11	Avonside	0-6-0ST	Avonside	1428	?	1901-c1925
	Jersey I	0-4-0ST	Fletcher Jennings	129	1873	1908-1949
	Jersey II	0-4-0ST	Fletcher Jennings	139	1874	1908-1949
	Jersey III	0-4-0ST	Fletcher Jennings	150	1875	1908-1949
A more detailed table of these locomotives is included in Appendix B.						

Locomotives and Rolling Stock

Table 7. *Diesel traction used in the works 1947 – 1974*

Name	Builder	Type	Stock number	Dates used
Forward	John Fowler	4-wheel diesel mech	3900012	1947 – 1970
Advance	John Fowler	4-wheel diesel mech	3900037	1949 – 1970
Efficiency	John Fowler	4-wheel diesel mech	3900048	1951 – 1974
	Ruston & Hornsby		435398	1959 – 1972
Efficiency	Ruston & Hornsby		446207	1961 – 1971
	Ruston & Hornsby	Used as spares	435393	1959 – 1969
	Ruston & Hornsby		518187	1965 - 1971

Table 8. *Motive power used for standard gauge working*

Name	Builder	Type	Comments
	Fordson	4-wheel diesel mech	Basically a converted tractor. [1]
No. 79	Manning Wardle	0-6-0 ST	1888 model – bought 1925
Mersey	Black Hawthorn	0-4-0 ST	1892 model – bought 1925
Progress	John Fowler	0-4-0 diesel mech	Bought new in 1945
Peter	John Fowler	0-4-0 diesel mech	1940 model – bought 1950
	Ruston & Hornsby	4-wheel diesel mech	1960 model – bought 1975

1. E.A. Holwill tells us that this tractor was coupled up to about 5 standard gauge wagons to test its capabilities and when it was started off, it lifted off its wheels – presumably the front ones!   It would seem that it was in fact on site for only a few days and then did nothing whilst it was there, following this initial debacle.

were also used on one of the other two locomotives, but this is unclear. However from photographic evidence it is certain that a riveted cylindrical tank was used on at least one of them.   The conversion work was undertaken by Messrs. Hodges of Exeter in 1910, 1915 and 1914 respectively.   The first and second conversions are believed to have been carried out at Peters Marland, and the third at Hodges' own works.

The narrow gauge continued in the works and the clay fields for many years after the demise of the "main line", and diesel traction was used in later years as shown in Table 7.

Standard (4ft 8½in) gauge was introduced to the works at the opening of the North Devon & Cornwall Junction Light Railway for shunting main line wagons, and a variety of motive power was used as shown in Table 8.

Rolling Stock

It was noted earlier that J.B. Fell was in close touch with most of the reputable locomotive builders of the day, and the same is true of rolling stock builders.   We have no evidence as to who built the wagons for the Aldershot War Office trial railway, but for the Pentewan line, it seems that these were built in the company's own workshops to the design of J.M. Rendel, the consulting engineer for the Pentewan conversion. For his Mont Cenis line however, Fell had had a test coach made by the Metropolitan Carriage & Wagon Company, and although they were not to gain the contract for the operating stock, Fell must have kept in touch with them, for in 1880 they were awarded the contract for the wagons for the Torrington & Marland.

The Bill of Quantities (Appendix C) in the contract provides again in the briefest of words, for "20 wagons @ £45 each = £900.0.0d."   As we saw earlier, the specification notes that the axle loading for both locomotives and wagons was 2 tons, so the tare weight of the wagons would be 4 tons. This would allow a capacity of between 3 and 3½ tons. (The makers drawing shows a capacity of 3 tons.)   The wagons were of a basic, but sturdy design and as such, capable of

Opposite page top: "Jersey II" with a cylindrical tender tank. (Frank Jones)

Opposite page bottom: "Jersey II" out of use in 1951, probably awaiting scrapping. (Frank Jones)

maintenance and repair by the Clay Company's own employees on site. The wagons were equipped with centre buffers and side chains, and brakes were fitted on one side only, although as with the Avonside locomotive, the drawing shows a central "chopper" type of coupling/buffer. The wagons were numbered, some in the centre of the side, some at the right hand end. With so few photographs to study, it is not possible to determine whether the system was to use the centre or end of the side, or whether this was changed at some date.

The 1892 prospectus itemises 9 wagons in the clay works and 40 on the railway, a total of 49. Whether the 9 in the works were used for transport of clay up the line to Torrington is not clear, but obviously the original 20 had by then been supplemented by a similar number of additional vehicles to cater for the increased transport of clay and other materials on the railway. Records indicate a further 10 wagons ordered in 1895 and 1902 respectively, and it may be assumed that these were repeat orders from earlier and that probably the extra 20 were similarly ordered between 1880 and 1892.

The July 1913 report of the correspondent of *The Locomotive* mentions "nearly 100 wagons – most built at Marland". Presumably by this time the Marland Company's employees were turning their hands to wagon building as well as running repairs and conversions. This same report also mentions that the Company had hired some standard gauge wagons and these were running from Torrington to local LSWR stations. No doubt these were mainly for transhipment of clay from the narrow gauge wagons and onward to Fremington Docks for offloading onto the waiting ships. By the outbreak of World War II, it is understood that the Company had some 30 of these wagons on hire.

As the railway was ostensibly a freight only line, no provision was made for the carriage of passengers. However workmen's trains were operated on a daily basis and in the beginning they were carried in open trucks. At some point later, three vehicles were fitted with seats and covered in for this purpose, presumably by the Clay Company's own men at the works. One of these was of a longer wheelbase than normal and was also presumably altered on site. From a study of the few photographs available, it appears that these were lettered "NDCCo. Ltd". In 1909, two surplus double-decked horse trams were bought from the London County Council. These were converted to single deck and fitted with appropriate draw-gear to provide additional capacity on the line.

One of the covered trucks for workmen's transport. Seen here at Dunsbear on 15th June 1948. From its appearance it may well still have been in use at the time for running around the works and clay fields. (The late Jim Peden)

One of the ex-London Transport tramcars, used for carrying workmen to the works. The second car is seen coupled to the right. Photographed on 5th July 1912. (The late Jim Peden)

"Peter" with a train of wagons out in the clay fields.
Obviously posed; but nonetheless a delightful shot of the railway at work in its own environment. The crew are clearly proud of their charge, which appears in
pristine condition. Probably taken before 1900. (Tom Bartlett Postcard Collection, Berrynarbor, EX34 9SE)

Chapter 5

OPERATION

January 1881 thus saw the start of the little railway, which was to be a feature of life in the area for the next forty four years. Whilst the line was "officially" open, it is clear that not all the work had been completed, or at least not to everyone's satisfaction. On New Year's Day, a meeting of the Highway Board for the District of Great Torrington noted:

"...Also that the Marland Clay Company had laid the rails at the crossings of the roads, but that complaints were made of the unfinished state of the roads at the crossings and that single gates only had been placed at Watergate. The Clerk was directed to call the immediate attention of the Company to the subject and require the roads to be completed in a week and double gates to be placed at Watergate according to the original arrangement between the Company and the Board."

Mr Morley at the Rolle estate office was also busy early in the year, for on 8th Jan. 1881 he writes to

"G N Fell Esq. Torrington.
Dear Sir,
Thorne, the Rolle Road Toll-House Keeper, has been here this morning and tells me that you have seen the spot where the water, diverted by the Claymoor Railway, is at the present time damaging our Road. Thorne tells me that you wished him to make an estimate as to the cost of rectifying this, but he says he is unable to do this. Would it not be as well for the Company to do what is necessary? I have not seen the place myself but it is only a small matter I believe.
Yours faithfully, A L J Morley"

A few days later, on 12th January 1881, the estate office is writing to Fred Holwill:

"In accordance with your request sent by Mr Barrie, I send you the a/c of the timber purchased by the Marland Brick & Clay Company from the Rolle Estate and I shall be much obliged to you will kindly obtain an early settlement of same.
Yours truly, J Fairchild "

The Highway Board for the District of Great Torrington meet again on 29th January, having apparently received some satisfaction to their earlier problem:

"The Surveyor reported that the Marland Brick and Clay Company had promised to put up double gates at Watergate crossing as originally agreed on, and that they had placed ballast on the Coleford crossing and engaged to complete the roads to the Board's satisfaction."

As noted earlier, the weather had been exceptionally severe, with snow falling on and off since 18th January. It was obviously still causing trouble in the area for at the same meeting of the Highway Board on 29th January:

"The Surveyor reported that every exertion had been used to clear the main roads which were blocked by the recent snow storm and that application had been made for the clearance of several cross roads. A letter was read from the Chairman of the Board on the same subject. Proposed by Mr J Hooper, seconded by Mr Rowtcliff and carried – That the cost of clearing the roads blocked by snow be charged on the District fund. Proposed by Mr Rowtcliff, seconded by Mr Bonifant, and carried – That Two shillings a day be paid for such clearance. Proposed by Mr J. Hooper, seconded by Mr Norman and carried – That such roads be cleared as the Surveyor in his discretion may think necessary."

No doubt there were quite a few items on the "snagging list" for according to the account in the *North Devon Journal* of the official opening run on 5th February (quoted in Chapter 3) ballasting of the Marland end of the line was apparently still to be completed. Certainly this would seem to be supported by the letter previously referred to from the Rolle estate office to George Fell at the end of October agreeing to further excavations of stone from one of their quarries. A little later it will be seen from further correspondence that stone was still being sought for finishing the ballasting, but eventually all the outstanding work would have been completed, and the railway started to be accepted into the local way of life.

The route of the new railway ran from the Torridge valley up the Pencleave valley, past Drummet's Flour Mill, Langtree Mill and Langtree Farm to Stowford Moor where, at Yarde, there was a siding and a level crossing. Near Yarde was a passing loop at the summit of the line, which was the operational halfway point. Continuing over the turnpike road, the route followed the River Mere to Marland where, at Bury Moor, a goods depot and siding was established for the use of the local farmers and merchants. After the relative ease of the well-engineered extension to Torrington, the Torrington & Marland abounded with sharp curves and steep gradients – much more the cheaply built narrow gauge branch line. It was however a beautiful run through the wooded and unspoilt countryside.

Hugh Strong made a trip on the railway in about 1889 on his visit to the works, and in his book *Industries of North Devon* he gives a lovely description of the journey, which is worth quoting in part here.

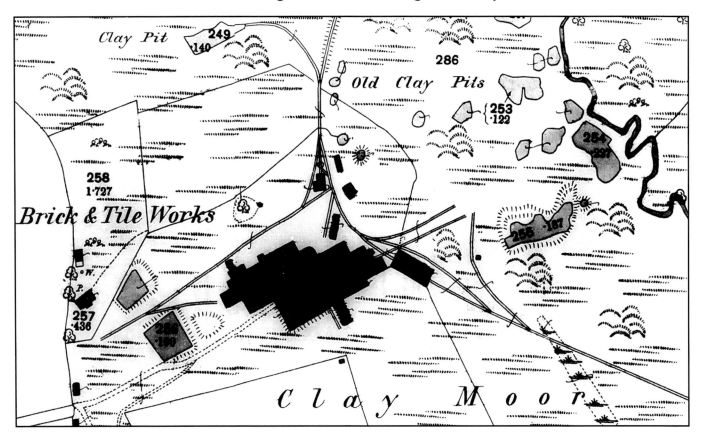

(Crown Copyright 25in to the mile 1st Edition)

"Through a famous hunting country, of which the Gribble Inn, a popular "meet", is the centre, we run to Yarde, a little hamlet less than a mile from the works, where a foreman's residence and sixteen workmen's cottages – built, of course, of Marland brick – have been erected for the accommodation of the employees. Between Yarde and Marland Clay Moor we pass Winscott, the pleasant residence of J.C. Moore-Stevens, Esq., that stands on a wooded eminence which overlooks the extensive property of the Squire. A gentle descent brings us to the entrance to the Moor. In the centre of over a hundred acres of clayey soil rises the tall stack of the works, and round it cluster the kilns and the workshops of Mr J.W. Ludlam, the enterprising proprietor of the industry, in whose hands it has been for six years. The works themselves, although most compactly arranged, cover three acres. They are situate in Marland parish, and lie in a hollow of the gently undulating country. A stream bounds the property and divides it from Merton parish, whose church spire on the hill-top above the works is gilded by the last rays of the departing sun."

The line actually started in Torrington as a siding between two of the LSWR's sidings in the goods yard. From here it passed under the main road by way of a short 20-yard tunnel lined with Marland Brick and this was used as a shed for the locomotive based at Torrington. A short run-round loop then followed, set in a 20 feet deep cutting, and then the line ran on to the bridge over the Rolle Road and thence on to the main viaduct some 40 feet above the Torridge. Running off the viaduct along a long trestle, the line started its climb past Drummett's Mill and up through the woods of the Pencleave Valley. At Watergate Bridge, just under two miles out, a short siding was provided, and what is now the B3227 road was crossed on the flat. Climbing steadily now, the line headed south-east up the valley, past Langtree Wick before swinging round to the south and back again over Stowford Moor. The summit of the climb was now reached, 4 miles and 12 chains out, and it was here that a passing loop was situated. Here the loaded wagons from the clay works were handed over to the Torrington engine in exchange for the empties back from Torrington goods yard. Turing east now, the line ran down hill to Yarde, where another short siding was placed by the road crossing. A short siding was to be found at Dunsbear after the line had passed over another minor road, and soon the line was entering the works area and the lines to the various clay workings split off.

As an extension of the local transport infrastructure, the railway could probably carry virtually any commodity except livestock. The Rolle Estate records show "building materials" being carried and this would certainly include timber in some form. The Estate records also show that gravel, bricks, lime and pipes were carried, and no doubt other goods would have been carried as and when required. Annual traffic in 1881 – the first year of operation – was said

The mine head and trains.
One of the Fletcher Jennings locomotives, possibly "Jersey II" or "Jersey III", probably some time between the wars. The train is apparently loading clay at the pithead. (The Beaford Archive)

Table 9. Light railway traffic 1898, 1899, and 1900

NDCC Ltd	1898	1899	1900
Clay	17,179	12,472	15,112
Brick	4,182	4,698	6,225
Coal	1,730	1,601	1,860
Gravel	178	336	31
Sundries	36	15	10
Public traffic			
Goods, manure, coal, etc.	2,652	2,714	2,410
Parcels & light goods	43	64	52
Total	**26,000**	**21,900**	**25,700**

to be 12,000 tons of clay, bricks, and coal, which had levelled to about 10,000 tons by the end of the decade. By the turn of the century the figure was running at about 25,000 tons per annum of clay, bricks, and agricultural produce, and in the early 1920s traffic had risen to some 42,000 tons. Public freight (that is, goods carried for other than the Clay Company) was estimated to be in the order of 3,000 tons in 1881 and up to 5,000 tons in 1909, although an annual figure

of around 2,500 tons is estimated to be the average. Records from the Clay Company give us firm figures for the 3 years 1898–1900 (shown in Table 9), and show a three year average of 24,533 tons.

Rates seem to vary considerably depending on the source, and have been quoted variously in the range from 1d to 6d per ton/mile. Reference again to the Rolle Estate records is helpful and interesting. Unfortunately there is only

The brickworks, circa 1893. (The Beaford Archive)

one entry, which gives the weight of the load, and assuming Watergate to be about two miles from Torrington we can calculate a rate of 7½d per ton/mile. Traffic receipts from public customers are shown in the records as being £550 in 1891 against operating expenses for the whole line of £915. In later years these figures were more in the region of £300 against £600-£700. The July 1913 article in *The Engineer* quotes the operating costs, excluding management expenses, of 1½d per ton/mile for the year 1911.

Six men were employed by the Clay Company at Torrington station to unload the clay into the wagons of the LSWR. It is also believed that two men were employed full time in maintenance work of the Torridge viaduct. Mr E.A. Holwill in his interview (described later in this chapter) says "about eight" men were employed at the station, so this would seem to be correct. At the station, the Company had an office and a shelter for the men. Three "rail packers" (presumably what we would call lengthsmen or permanent way men) were also employed with six locomotive men (three drivers and three assistants) catering for the motive power requirements. The locomotives were kept at Marland apart from one, which spent its nights in the little tunnel under the turnpike road just outside the station. It is thought that "Mary" and "Marland" were shedded at the works, while "Avonside" spent its nights at Torrington.

Official passenger services were restricted to the workmen's trains, the first of which left Torrington at about 6.25 or 6.30 in the morning. About 50 men boarded at Torrington, whilst 6 joined at Watergate and another 20 at Yarde. They alighted at the works, from whence they went into the works, or off to the pits; probably once more by train. At around 9 o'clock, the Torrington engine would return with the first load of clay, and thereafter another two or three trainloads would be dealt with during the day, depending upon production and demand. The last movement of the day would be at 6 o'clock in the evening when the workmen's train returned. Loaded clay trains from the works would wait at the summit loop near Yarde for the arrival of the next train of empties from Torrington. Usually trains were made up of four loaded wagons and one would be left at the summit loop whilst the locomotive returned for another. The two trains would then be marshalled together at the summit loop. The train of empties would be composed of eight wagons and the locomotives would swap trains at the loop, the Torrington engine returning with the loaded train and the Marland engine with empties. The average daily traffic of clay was said to be approximately 100 tons. This equates to 30 wagon loads at a nominal 3½ tons each – about 105 tons. These 30 wagons would be unloaded into about 10 of the LSWR's standard gauge 10-ton wagons.

"Avonside" takes a break.
A really evocative shot of "Avonside" in Watergate siding, sometime early in the 1900s, looking towards Torrington. The three gentlemen in shirt sleeves are probably the "rail packers" who attended to the line – permanent way men, as we would call them now. They appear to be attending to the main line by the bucket! Presumably "Avonside" has brought in some supplies for their work, or maybe is delivering goods for the Rolle Estate or a neighbouring farmer.
(Roger Kidner)

The Torrington & Marland Light Railway

As built, the original line ran for about ¼ mile on the clay moors to connect with the workings. By 1884 there was about ½ mile on the moors but in 1892 Lord Clinton leased further clay deposits on Bury Moor to the south-east of the works to the Company and another mile of line was added for this. A couple of sidings were added on the Moor for this purpose and also to serve Lord Clinton's estate at nearby Heanton Satchville.

Meanwhile, the Rolle estate office people were still busy, for on 5th February 1881 a letter addressed to Mr Fred Holwill, Torrington is concerned with payment for timber taken over two years earlier:

"Dear Sir,
Timber – Priestacott Wood, Frithelstock.

I find that three oak trees, delivered to Mr Robins, the Clerk of Works at Buckland Brewer, have been removed by your men in the above wood, along with the timber which was sold to you during 1878. The following are the numbers of the trees and I have added the measurements of them:

	Nos	Length	Girth	Feet	Inches
1	72	16	11	11	1
2	76	A.25	13	29	4
3	77	14	10	9	8
				50 feet	1 inch
				@ 1/3d = £3.2.6d.	

I think you will find the above correct, and I should be obliged if you would send me a cheque for the amount Viz.: £3. 2. 6d. Yours faithfully, A.L.J. Morley"

Exactly one week later, Mr Morley again writes to Fred Holwill, this time regarding stone for ballast:

"Mr F Holwill
Dear Sir,
I am sorry I was unable to reply yesterday to your letter of the 9th instant relative to the additional Ballast required by the Marland Brick Co., but I wished to speak to Mr Lipscomb first.
There is no objection to the Company taking the Ballast they require on the terms named in Mr Lipscomb's letter to Mr Fell of October 22nd 1880, provided they take it from the Quarry in the wood No. 1329 and do not go beyond the hedge on the N.W. side, nor in extending the quarry go beyond the lines of the present Quarry Thus:
(see below)

The piece of land marked A may be worked, but the Quarry may not be extended towards B and C. The arrangements as to the sloping of the Quarry, after the Ballast has been taken, must be the same as made in the letter referred to above.
The Forester informs me that several trees beyond those marked by him have been felled by the Company. Might I ask by what authority was this done? I should be glad to hear from you as soon as possible. Yours faithfully, A.L.J. Morley."

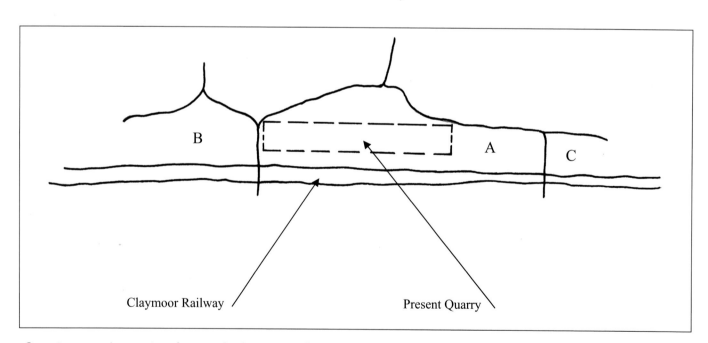

Opposite page: An amusing photograph of wagon number 33 – one of the second batch from the Metropolitan Carriage & Wagon Company – which appears to have been into the works for repair, or load testing!
(The Ball Clay Heritage Society)

Operation

It is clear from this correspondence that there was still work to be done to complete the railway, and indeed the press article on the opening of the line makes mention of ballasting at the further end of the line not yet being completed. The estate office was obviously kept in close touch with what was happening in the area.

Seemingly in response to a request from J.B. Fell regarding the proposed Hatherleigh – Okehampton line, Mr Morley responded on 15th February 1881:

"Dear Sir,
I have spoken to Mr Rolle this morning on the subject of your enquiry as to whether he had the Plans of the line the proposed Railway between Hatherleigh and Okehampton was to take when the route was surveyed some ten or twelve years ago. He wishes me to say that he believes his solicitors have these Plans, but that he does not feel justified in producing them without consulting the other Landowners at whose expense these costly Plans were made.
Yours faithfully,
A.L.J. Morley"

Routine contractual and accounting matters seem to be still occupying Mr Morley and a brief note on 27th May 1881 to the Company Secretary of the Clay Company enquires:

"J. Groves Cooper, Esq.
Wear Gifford
Dear Mr Cooper,
Mr Holwill informs me that the timber a/c which we have against the Marland Brick & Clay Company should be sent to you. I therefore enclose it and if I have done wrong please let me know to whom I ought to send it.
Yours very truly,
A.L.J. Morley"

On 10th June a further letter to J. Groves Cooper, from Mr Lipscomb, raises important tenancy questions, matters regarding the still incomplete detail of the railway, (and sets the imagination running wild).

"Dear Sir,
The Marland Clay Company are in occupation of the sheds near the Rolle Road Toll Gate at Taddiport. I must either have possession or an arrangement as to rent. The only use which the Company is now making of the sheds is as a Depot

MARLAND BRICK WORKS,

Torrington,

June 23rd, 1900.

DEAR SIR,

In consequence of the increased cost of Coals we are obliged to raise our prices, and annex the list which will be in force from to-day.

Hoping to be favoured with your further orders, which will receive careful and prompt attention,

We remain,

Yours faithfully,

For The North Devon Clay Co., Ltd.,
Proprietors,

Henry Holwill,
Manager.

⊱ PRICE LIST. ⊰

June 23rd, 1900.

	per 1,000.	Approx. Weight per 1,000. Tons. Cwt.	
Best Pressed Buff Facings	65/-	3	0
Seconds do. do.	55/-	"	
Moulded do. ... from	75/-	"	
Keystones, &c.			
Selected Wire Cut Facings	45/-	"	
„ Perforated do.	42/6	2	8
Common Wire Cuts	37/6	3	0
„ Perforated	32/6	2	8
Pressed Engineering Brick	50/-	3	0
Wire Cut do.	40/-	"	
Culvert and Arch Brick, &c.			
Best Pressed " Salmon " Facings ...	65/-	"	
„ „ " Red " „ ...	55/-	"	
Fire Brick, Best	65/-		
„ Seconds	55/-		
Best Buff (Stable and Paving) 9 x 4½ x 2.	60/-	2	15
Brindled do.	55/-	"	
Seconds do.	50/-	"	

TERMS :—Three Months Credit, or 5 % Discount for Monthly Accounts (i.e. Payments on or before 15th of Month after date of Invoice.) Interest charged on overdue Accounts.

The brickworks price list and letter.
Prices increases are apparently nothing new!
(Author's collection)

for storage of some old Trucks, some corn, salt, etc., and a Stallion (whose public performances on the premises are complained of by the modest women of the neighbourhood). Can the Company give me possession at Midsummer, paying some acknowledgement for the current quarter's occupancy, or do they wish to hold the place on?

I have also to ask when the Watergate Siding is to be put in? Also when the fencing is to be completed at Watergate (or Langtree) Mills?

Yours faithfully, R H Lipscomb"

A couple of weeks later, on 26th June 1881, the *Bideford Gazette* takes up the cudgels again in the name of railway progress. In a lengthy article it presses the argument for an extension of the railway southwards, possibly to Launceston. It is interesting to read these articles and see how the press of the day went to great lengths to champion the cause of railway development where it felt it was justified. The language and phraseology may appear overtly patronising and flowery at times but they certainly must have got their

message across, even if the sought after extension did not materialise for many years. Unfortunately, as commented upon later, the talk here is of a connection to Launceston through Halwill Junction rather than the more direct and potentially much more beneficial route to Okehampton or Sampford Courtenay.

Returning to matters of railway operation, extracts taken from the Clay Company's annual reports (shown in Table 10) provide us with further useful data on business with sales and profit/loss figures for the later 1890s.

It would seem from this that, whilst trade generally was improving, the costs of running and maintaining the railway were proving an ongoing problem to the Company. Concern was being shown at the state of repair of some of the viaducts after the Great War, during which maintenance had no doubt been pared to the bone, if indeed any at all had been carried out. It is believed that in about 1913 the bridge over the Rolle Road (the path of the old Rolle Canal), which led on to the Torridge Viaduct, was replaced by an iron girder span, and from time to time additional timbers were added for

Operation

Table 10. Total annual sales (tons) from the Clay Company's annual reports			
Year	Clay	Bricks	Profit (loss)
1894	6,900	-	(£1,444.11.5d)
1895	10,100	309,000	£109.7.10d
1896	14,850	613,000	£640.5.5d [1]
1897			£243.14.5d [2]

1. Includes provision for an estimated liability of £70 in connection with the Okehampton Railway scheme.
2. Includes heavy expenditure on railway, rolling stock and machinery.

A rake of wagons loaded with clay awaits its turn in the transfer shed.
(The Ball Clay Heritage Society)

support. After the War, in about 1921, both Stowford Moor viaduct and the Torridge viaduct at Torrington were considerably strengthened with timber and iron. J.B. Fell's son, George Noble Fell, was consulted on these works, thus maintaining the Fell connection.

Mr Maurice Dowson, who supplied much of the information of the clay workings, mentioned the old timber viaduct of the Torrington & Marland, which in his time had no handrails at all, and recalls being told of the occasional derailment on the viaduct. The men would quite happily walk out on to the viaduct with jacks and perform the re-railing operation! However it appears that many people would not walk out over the viaduct in view of its height and narrow width. Looking back at the *Gazette* article on the inaugural run in February 1881, it was noted that:

"the feeling of jollity suddenly changed to one of wonder and tremulation – wonder that engineering skill could devise so light a structure combined with safety, and tremulation lest the one thought uppermost in the minds of all should be

One of the drying sheds, with piles of clay drying out prior to shredding. The very simple and basic construction of the wagons is evident in this shot.
(The Ball Clay Heritage Society)

realised. A looker-on from the common above afterwards informed us that the movement of the train across the viaduct as he looked down upon it presented the appearance of a party of children being conveyed across a toy bridge in perambulators."

The question of whether the Torridge viaduct was actually fitted with handrails is one that has been raised elsewhere. Photographs exist showing handrails all along its length, handrails at each end only, and no handrails at all! It has been suggested that this was the work of a photographers retouching brush, but this seems to be rather a fanciful idea. It is to be noted that the correspondent of the *North Devon Journal* notes in his piece on the opening run, that the bridge leading on to the viaduct had "no side rails". Presumably he means handrails. This could be taken to imply that the Viaduct itself did have such rails. The most likely explanation, based on the dates and chronology of the various photographs, is that the original full-length handrail was

gradually removed over the years.

Mr Dowson also spoke of the Yarde viaduct and remembers being told that in the early days of the railway, the then manager of the clay works ordered waste clay, etc to be taken out and tipped under the viaduct to fill it in. This was done gradually over a period and probably to more than one. Presumably this had a twofold reason: to get rid of otherwise problematic waste, and to gradually remove the need for maintaining the timber viaducts. Discrepancies in the lengths of some of the viaducts between different editions of the Ordnance Survey maps from the end of the nineteenth century and early part of the twentieth would tend to be thus explained.

The land rented from The Hon Mark Rolle appears to have been charged at an annual figure of £12.10.0d, and from a study of the Estate account books, it seems that rental first became due from 1st February 1880, which is presumably the date on which J.B. Fell and the Green Odd Company took over the land for final surveying and marking out prior to

A very early view of the railway running into the works yard. The brickworks dominate this view – note the stacks of clay drainpipes on the right – whilst someone takes their ease in the foreground.
(The Ball Clay Heritage Society)

actually starting work on the railway.

The first entry in the accounts appears in the 1882 account book as "from 1st February 1880 @ £12.10.0d. p.a. : £26.17.0d. is the rent from that time to Lady Day 1882. Due 1883 £10.13.0d." The mathematics of this calculation rather evades me as I calculate the period to be 2 years and 53 days, which would give a rent for that first period of nearer £25.16.0d. The £10.13.0d. is also confusing not just to me, as we shall see.

The entry in the 1884 account book reads "Paid £10.13.0d., thus arrears of £1.17.0d." The following year's entry shows matters evidently resolved to the Estate's satisfaction: "Due £12.10.0d. plus arrears of £1.17.0d. – paid £14.7.0d." Examination of the surviving account books of the period do not show any other anomalies, other than in five odd years where it seems that as well as the annual payment, the railway paid another half "on account" until the next Lady

Day.

No details are available to us today of what rents the other landowners were charging, but no doubt they would be in keeping with the levels charged by the Rolle estate.

On Tuesday, 7th February 1882, the *Bideford Gazette* reported excitedly on the visit of a group of dignitaries and foreign guests to Torrington:

"DISTINGUISHED VISIT to the MARLAND LIGHT RAILWAY.
It is now about twelve months ago since we first had the privilege of taking a trip over the Light Railway which runs from Torrington Station, at the terminus of the North Devon Railway to Peters Marland Brickworks, a distance of 6½ miles. Mr. G.N. Fell, the eminent engineer, who has conquered Mont Cenis (sic) is the constructor of the line, and he was on Wednesday honoured by a visit from Mr Fung

Yee, the Chinese Vice-Minister in London and Secretary of the Chinese Legation, and a company of other gentlemen interested in railway work. The Chinese Minister was accompanied by Major Grover R.E. from the War Office; Mr H. Beverige jun., Teintain (China), Mr. Woodall (Dudley), Mr Joseph Wright (Birmingham), Mr Fell, senr., and Mr Fell jun.. It was expected that the Japanese Ambassador would have been present as well, but he was unavoidable prevented from coming. The object of the visit of the Chinese Minister was to report to his Government on the construction and working of the light railway with a view to introducing the system into China."

This visit would have had two particularly attractive aspects for the Fells; firstly the prospects of interesting the Chinese in building a patent Fell railway in their country, and secondly rekindling the interest of the War Office by showing them a fully operational railway using Fell's patent system. A bonus was to have been the inclusion of the Japanese Ambassador in the party, but he was unavoidably prevented from coming. An earlier visit some weeks previously by Sir Harry Parkes and Sir Douglas Forsyth had been made with Japanese development in mind, but this enquiry does not appear to have been furthered.

The Torrington Highways Board were on the trail of the Clay Company again in 1883, for at their meeting on 27th January, "The Clerk was directed to call the attention of the Marland Company to the want of gates at the Coleford Crossing, and to the irregularity in closing the gates at the Yard and Watergate Crossings."

At their meeting a month later on 24th February, the Board were seemingly unhappy with the Clay Company's response, for their minutes read:

"A letter was read from the Manager of the Marland Brick and Clay Works in reply to the Clerk's letter respecting the crossings, and the Clerk was directed to inform him that the statements in his letter were incorrect, the gates at Yard being out of order, and the Chairman having lately passed Watergate when the gate was open and sticking across the road."

Matters of rent and accounting were again to the fore in February 1884, for on the 13th, a letter to "Mr H Holwill for The Marland Brick & Clay Company" makes the request:

"Dear Sir,
Please send a cheque for £7.1.9d. in settlement of the enclosed a/c after deducting the year's rent of £12.10.0d. due by you to the Rolle Estate on the 1st instant. I enclose a receipt for the rent and I shall be much obliged by your receipting and returning your account.
Yours obediently,
J Fairchild
For R.H. Lipscomb"

Money is again on the agenda on 14th April 1885 for "The Manager, Marland Brick & Clay Company, Torrington" is asked:

"Dear Sir,
Clay Moor Railway.
Please send me cheque for £12.10.0d. in payment of the year's rent due to the Rolle Estate on 1st February last. If you prefer to pay the rent until Lady Day last please add £1.17.0d.
Yours obdtly.
J. Fairchild
for R.H. Lipscomb"

This does not seem to have had the desired effect, for on 23rd June, Mr Fairchild writes:

"The Manager, Marland Clay Works, Torrington.
Dear Sir,
Clay Moor Railway.
I should be glad to receive your cheque for £14.7.0d. in settlement of the rent due to the Rolle Estate at Lady Day last. If you make any deduction for Income Tax you must please send me your Income Tax receipt.
Yours truly,
J Fairchild
for R.H. Lipscomb"

Developments in the area were being considered as time went by, and at the monthly meeting of the Torrington Town Council on 18th May 1888:

"The Surveyor produced a plan for the proposed extension of the footpath to the Railway Station. Proposed by Mr Chapple seconded by Mr Jones and carried unanimously – That the work be carried out under the direction of the Highway Committee, provided the necessary money be granted at a Joint Meeting, and that the London and South Western Railway and the Marland Company's are willing to bear their share of the expense."

The Council were no doubt somewhat "miffed" at their meeting on 6th June 1888 when they were advised:

"A letter was read from the Secretary to the Marland Clay Company stating that the Company regret that they cannot assist in the work of making a better footpath to the Railway Station, but that the fencing around their cutting should be renewed forthwith."

Quite how that point was resolved is not known, but on 17th December 1888 the Council "Meeting was advised that Messrs Bircham & Co had produced a plan for the proposed station approach".

At this time the pressure was again mounting for a standard gauge railway extension southwards and the

A lovely shot taken from on board a loaded train on its way to Torrington. The train engine appears to be "Mary".
(The Ball Clay Heritage Society)

Torrington & Okehampton Railway was soon to gain its Act of Incorporation. It would seem that the clay and brick companies were also pushing for extensions, but to their own narrow gauge line. A document drafted by the Clay Company sets out the scope of the operations at Marland and, as well as giving details of the plant employed, provides a interesting insight into how the railway was perceived by them. It is undated, but must have been produced around 1892, and gives some detail of the operations at Peters Marland. It splits operations into three sections: "The Clay Works, the Brick Works and the Railway (which serves the other two)". A description of the clay and its uses is followed by reference to "about 1½ miles of Railway (independent of the main line mentioned under the Railway department), two locomotives, 9 wagons, Traction Engine, 9 LSWR Trucks 4ft 8½in gauge, sheds and stores at the works. Station and place for shipment. Hoisting engines and gear at each mine. (The Railway Department has two locomotives as well)." The description of the brickworks is mainly devoted to an inventory of the buildings, plant and machinery.

The railway is mentioned in some detail, and concludes: "By extending the line to join the LSWR at Okehampton or Hallwell (sic) Junctions, (the present Line forming about half the length required) – the distance between Torrington and Plymouth would be reduced very considerably (nearly 50 miles) and consequently Bideford, Barnstaple, Ilfracombe, and North Devon generally would be brought into much better communication with South Devon and Cornwall than now exists, which would also benefit the Works and enlarge the area for the sale of goods, coal, &c., still retaining the monopoly." It is clear from this that the owners of the Torrington & Marland were seeking an extension of their own narrow gauge line here – possibly this was part of a prospectus to raise capital for the new company (North Devon Clay Company) about to be formed.

Life on the Torrington & Marland, and at the clay company, took its course with brick production being much in demand for water and sewerage works, the linings of bank strong rooms in London and elsewhere, and the construction of bridges and viaducts. Of the latter, the most important locally is Chelfam Viaduct on the old narrow gauge Lynton & Barnstaple Railway. This splendid monument to Victorian engineering still stands today.

The Torrington & Marland Light Railway

During the First World War, Torrington station saw much hay and timber traffic for war supplies, there being an artillery training area on Torrington Commons. Otherwise the line saw little change over the years, although it must have suffered, like everywhere else in the country, from labour shortages during the Great War.

At this stage, the memoirs of a member of the Holwill family make interesting reading. E.A. Holwill (nephew to Henry Holwill) was born in Southbourne near Bournemouth in 1905. His father was in the furniture trade. His uncle Henry suggested that the young E.A. Holwill join the Clay Company, and on 23rd January 1923, at the age of 18, he arrived in Torrington and went to work in the Company's offices at Peters Marland. In an interview in his later years, Mr Holwill gives us some insight into the operation of the railway and the works when he was employed there.

"They bought me a bicycle and twice a day I would have to go to Torrington Station as the clay from Peters Marland came in on the light railway, and each truck held 3½ tons. They'd bring this trainload in and the 3ft gauge line was in between the main lines and the sidings. We had a gang of about eight men at the station and they would heave the clay from the little trucks to the big trucks. I had a list of orders for the goods office at the station to tell the Clerk where the trucks had to go. They would make out labels for each truck. If we were shipping at Fremington (rather than Bideford) there was no telephone communication from Fremington, the only communication was the signal box phone on the private railway. So I would go down to the signal box and ring up the captain of a ship at Fremington who wanted to speak to me, or anything like that, otherwise the boat would arrive at Fremington Quay to collect about 350 tons of clay and they would send a telegram to say they'd arrived. I'll tell you of one telegram that I should have had framed, it said 'Mary Ellen in berth having her bottom scraped clean'! That was the only way they could communicate to know the ship was in and send the loads off otherwise costs could be incurred on the railway trucks. That went on all the time and our light railway was a good form of transport for people living out in the country. We used to be able to send out all sorts of things; to Lord Clinton for instance at his mansion, and a great deal of basic slag, a common fertiliser in those days, to local farmers, and also coal. Farmers and various others would order goods for Torrington station. The station would reconsign it and we delivered it to the various consignees. Then I would write out postcards and send them to the various people saying their goods were at Bury Moor station awaiting collection. The postcards would arrive next morning – that's with ½ penny stamps!

"We used to supply seventy five percent of all the English ball clay shipped. We had about one hundred and eighty men working at the mines when I started. There were nine mines with five men in each and one on top on the winch. Then there was the open pit producing clay for the brickyard as well, but after that closed we went down to ninety five men. Then we closed all the mines and opened up new pits with modern machinery and our staff went down to thirty five. That excludes administrative staff. Output went from 33,000 to over 100,000 tons. When I was there I only had a works manager and a works foreman, myself and a clerk in the office. The war took my pit foreman. I had a mines foreman but nobody in the office. Torridge Vale (the local dairy) used to lend me a girl to help out.

"Mr Wren built the cottages at Yard Halt and the manager of the brickworks lived in the big one at the bottom, called Yard Villa. There were sixteen cottages used by our workers. The brickworks operated up to the beginning of the First World War then stopped as the workers were all called up and the works closed. It then operated up to 1946 right through the War, but we were weren't making bricks then, we were making drainpipes and we supplied all the pipes for the Winkleigh Aerodrome but in 1946 we had a big slip in the pit; too much to clear away and that virtually closed the brickworks.

"We used to supply seventy five percent of all the English ball clay shipped to America from South Devon, Dorset and North Devon. We had an American buyer came one day in the 1930s with his shipping agent – a Mr Simpson! It was Mr Simpson of the Mrs Simpson!! (The husband of Wallis Simpson who later became Duchess of Windsor.) We shipped clay to Norway, Sweden, Denmark, France, Belgium, Holland, Italy and Greece and also to Australia and New Zealand and all over the world. During WWII we were able to ship to America because the Liberty Ships came over with supplies and used to go back with clay as ballast.

"I became Manager of the works in 1936 and we moved the office we had in South Street in Torrington to the works at the same time. Prior to that I did a lot of travelling, including two longs trips to the continent. I had three weeks in Poland and got out just three weeks before the War started.

"In 1967 we merged, by agreement, with Watts Blake Bearne of Newton Abbott."

When O.V.S. Bulleid of the Southern Railway introduced his West Country class of air smoothed pacific locomotives, number 34031 (originally 21C131) was allocated the name TORRINGTON. The naming ceremony was performed at the station on 24th November 1949 by none other than Mr Holwill, in his role as Mayor of Torrington.

Another action shot of clay en-route to Torrington. "Jersey II" or "Jersey III" is in charge this time. The driver or fireman, who is hanging on, seems very interested in something off scene. (The Ball Clay Heritage Society)

A survey party at Yarde.

A group of surveyors working on the line at Yarde opposite the row of cottages. The gate of the level crossing over the road can be seen in the background. The Marland line's short siding here was between the two men on the right of the picture and the gate. The original of the photograph is marked No 1, and is obviously one of a group that includes those of "Gyp" and "Bunty" working on the construction of the NDCJLR. These other two photographs are marked No 3 and No 4 respectively, in the same hand. Construction of the line commenced in 1922 and it was opened in July 1925 so the photographs probably date from between late 1922 and 1924, judging from the stage of construction reached in No 4 and the early work being carried out in this view. In July 1926, a year after the opening, a short platform and small shelter were provided here, on the left of the line as seen. The nature of the two buildings with sloping roofs on either side of the line is unknown; certainly there were gone soon after the NDCJLR opened.

(Author's collection/Spencer Taylor)

Chapter 6

AFTER THE NARROW GAUGE

The story of the Torrington & Marland Light Railway as an operational railway is virtually over, and it would have been possible to conclude our story with a brief note explaining that, in 1925, standard gauge rails finally pushed south from Torrington and connected up at Halwill Junction to the rest of the network. That would really not do the old T&M justice, for subsequent events need to be told in order to complete the "broad canvas" mentioned in the preface of this book. Also bringing the story of Torrington and its railways up to date does in some way bring us full circle. And so we return to the years at the turn of the twentieth century.

The opening of the Torrington & Marland did not satisfy the public demand for railway connection to the south, and several different plans were mooted in an attempt to achieve this goal. After lengthy discussion and argument, the Torrington & Okehampton Railway was incorporated on 6th July 1895 to run down the route of the Torrington & Marland, through Hatherleigh and join up with the LSWR at Fatherford, east of Okehampton. It would be single track with a passing loop at Hatherleigh. The North Devon Clay Company had opposed the Bill on the grounds that their railway met the needs of the area, and particularly it's own needs. They were naturally concerned that they might lose control of their transport and have to pay market rates. They eventually withdrew their opposition when clauses were included in the Bill protecting their rights and on receipt of £1,000 deposit towards the purchase price of the Torrington & Marland Railway. They were not working alone to protect their interests as, during 1894 and 1895, Henry Holwill was in correspondence with J.B. Fell via his son George Noble Fell who was advising them on their best course of action in fighting their corner.

The new Company was required to provide passenger services for the NDCC's employees at reasonable times and fares, and not to interfere with the working of the clay railway. One assumes that this latter referred to the period of construction. The LSWR agreed in 1896 to work the new line and the requisite Act of Parliament received Royal approval on 6th July 1895. An initial flurry of construction work then ensued but stopped again soon afterwards. A Parliamentary extension of time was granted in 1989 but financial difficulties abounded and no further work was done. In 1901 a further Parliamentary extension of time was granted and the title of the Company was changed to the much more impressive Plymouth and North Devon Direct Junction Railway, but this had no effect on the financial attractiveness of the Company. Of the £250,000 capital authorised, the Company had only been able to raise £28,000 and all this had gone. In 1904 the LSWR's General Manager reported to his Traffic Committee that the P&NDDJR would not be able to generate a reasonable revenue and that they should not therefore guarantee interest payments, as they were required to do. The LSWR consequently successfully applied for an Act of Abandonment, which was passed in 1907.

At this stage it is pertinent to consider the term "Light Railway" as it affects our story. There was no official definition of a light railway although the objective of such is clear; to open up a rural or undeveloped area at minimal cost. Certainly lower standards of engineering would be used, and requirements as to signalling, stations, level crossings and the like would be minimal. These allowances would be balanced by restrictions to train speeds and weight of locomotives and rolling stock. It was not until the Railway Construction Facilities Act of 1864 that such relaxation in standards of construction, etc, was allowed, and the first official use of the term "light railway" did not occur until the 1868 Regulation of Railways Act. There was however a national feeling that some official encouragement should be given to the promotion of light railways in order to facilitate the opening up of those areas not yet provided with railway connections and the 1896 Light Railways Act made provision for the authorisation of such lines without the need for Parliamentary approval.

The question of a railway link southwards festered locally for a few years and local interests then promoted the North Devon & Cornwall Junction Light Railway to link Torrington with Halwill Junction some 20½ miles away on the North Cornwall line of the LSWR. At this stage there entered upon the scene one of the greatest characters of the light railway era, Colonel Holman Frederick Stephens who, from his headquarters in Tonbridge, Kent, ran an empire of small railways throughout the land.

The North Devon Clay Company was not particularly enamoured at the idea of their railway being replaced by a larger entity, which would charge them for the carriage of their clay and other goods and initially they objected to the new proposals. They claimed, amongst other things, that their line catered adequately for the local community and a new line was not necessary. Considerable correspondence passed between them (in the shape of Fred Holwill and Colonel Stephens) on the subject, and meeting between the two parties took place. Eventually however they came round and settled down to argue the best terms for the sale of their line and to ensure that their interests would be protected in the setting up of any new line. Stephens had written to the North Devon Clay Company on 24th May 1905, suggesting that a third rail be laid alongside the existing track to allow the running of standard gauge trains through from Torrington and onwards to a new destination, probably at Okehampton.

Andersons' locomotive "Gyp".
Andersons, the contractors for the NDCJLR line, filled in some of the Fell trestles as part of their contract. This view is
understood to be at Yarde during filling in of the viaduct.
(Author's collection /Spencer Taylor)

This proposal did not get taken up. However, when the ND&CJLR was under construction, a third rail was laid at 3 feet gauge to allow the clay works trains to use the new line.

Colonel Stephens now provided the driving force behind the new venture and personally negotiated finance and would oversee the construction of the railway. In November 1909, application was made for a Light Railway Order under the 1896 Act and the Commissioners met on 28th February 1910, but it was not until January 1913 that they issued their approval. The new Company was incorporated on 28th August 1914. The Order contained several clauses designed to protect the NDCC's interests, the chief of which are reproduced here.

"30 (1) The Company shall…construct and thereafter maintain such efficient and temporary works as shall enable the Clay Company to carry on their traffic without interruption over the existing railway during the construction of the works of the Company and until the railway shall be completed and ready for the carriage of the Clay Company's traffic…"

"(2) The Company shall before the opening of the railway at their own expense construct and so long as the Clay Company shall continue to send traffic over the same for conveyance on the railway maintain and in proper working order a siding of not less than two hundred yards in length… and the Clay Company shall have the right at their own expense to make connection on their own land with such siding and to convey the Company's trucks to their works for the purposes of loading and unloading traffic."

"(4) The Company shall supply waggons as required and duly provide for the conveyance of the Clay Company's traffic and shall stop at least one train per day each way at the said siding for the accommodation thereof and in addition the Company

After the Narrow Gauge

Right: The new bridge under the construction at Torrington Station. The new bridge at the end of the station, built to allow the railway to run through the hillside to reach the river. The old bridge, or tunnel, for the Marland line still exists a few yards away to this day. It appears to have been bricked up part way in, but has become home to a colony of bats and is therefore protected from restoration or exploration.
(The Beaford Archive)

Below: The new road bridge over the River Torridge.
Part of the work necessary for the new railway bridge was a realignment of the road past the station on to a new bridge over the river. This is seen here under construction in 1925/6. The new bridge sits between the railway viaducts and the old Rothern road bridge.
(The Beaford Archive)

The Torrington & Marland Light Railway

Examples of the correspondence between George Fell and others regarding the Torrington & Okehampton Railway proposals. Some of these from Fell were written on Snaefell Mountain Railway stationery, as shown here.

shall on the request of the Clay Company stop any goods train beyond such daily train for the purpose of taking up not less than five loaded trucks."

"(6) The Company shall from and after the opening of the railway for public traffic convey the workmen and servants of the Clay Company to and from the said siding from and to Torrington Station and any other intermediate places to be agreed at reasonable times and fares regard being had to the number of workmen to be carried and to the usual hours of labour at the Clay Company's works and to the usual practice of railway companies in the matter of the issue of workmen's tickets at reduced fares."

The North Devon Clay Company had wanted £25,000 to sell the Torrington & Marland, but eventually after a lot of pressure agreed a figure of £18,000, of which £14,000 would be in NDCJLR shares. The First World War intervened to prevent anything further being done, but the powers under the Order did not lapse, and following cessation of hostilities, the North Devon & Cornwall Junction Light Railway (Amendment) Order was approved on 12th April 1922. This was mainly concerned with the financial details of the Company.

A meeting of the Torrington Town Council on 7th December 1921 considered the matter of whether to provide financial support to the proposed Torrington – Halwill railway. Details of terms for borrowing and repayment of loans were discussed. A proposal was made to subscribe the sum of £100 towards the Railway in order to show that they were in favour of the scheme and give it their moral support. This was defeated on amendment that the matter be deferred to the next meeting when more details could be considered. It appears that the Town Council did not subscribe, but Torrington Rural Council apparently put up £12,000.

A capital investment of some £300,000 was raised by Government grants and contributions from local and county authorities, local landowners (£10,000), the North Devon Clay Company (£9,000) and a few other donations. An additional factor that assisted in the launch of this new venture was the unemployment position in North Devon at that time. It was recorded that in 1922 the unemployment figures locally were: Barnstaple – 700, Bideford – 600 and Torrington – 105. Additionally some 200 agricultural labourers were not registered with the Labour Exchange. It was hoped that between 80% and 90% could be employed on the new railway construction work.

After the Narrow Gauge

The new viaduct from the hillside above.
The NDCJLR's new viaduct, looking out towards Watergate, probably only a few years after coming into use. The old track bed of the Torrington and Marland can be seen to the left. The photographer would have been standing just above the old Marland line tunnel out of the station. (Tom Bartlett Postcard Collection, Berrynarbor, EX34 9SE)

Freight traffic was naturally seen as the prime source of income for the line, based on an anticipated annual amount of clay of between 40,000 and 50,000 tons, plus that from the new clay works at Meeth. Cattle and livestock traffic was also expected to be of importance, as was coal from South Wales and the tourist trade. The picturesque nature of north and central Devon was expected to draw a large number of holidaymakers and sightseers. Very prophetically, the then Minister of Transport, Sir Eric Geddes, made a speech on 17th March 1919 regarding the development of motor transport that can almost be regarded as being government policy ever since. "I think that we must look to the development of motor traction for our agricultural areas." Local roads were hardly in a fit state to take the relatively small vehicles then operating, let alone the giant articulated vehicles of today!

The appointed contractors were P&W Anderson Ltd of Glasgow, and Mr Arthur Neale MP, Parliamentary Secretary to the Ministry of Transport, cut the first sod at Lewer Bridge, near Hatherleigh on 30th June 1922. The total mileage of the line was to be 20½ miles, with a construction period estimated at 20 months. Work commenced at the southerly end of the line, but later in the year, the North Devon Clay

Company agreed that Andersons could use the Torrington & Marland for construction purposes, provided that they did not interfere with clay traffic to and from Torrington station. This point was to prove a bone of contention on several occasions over the next year or two.

It is not clear how many of the local unemployed were taken on for the work, although we know that the Bideford and Torrington labour exchanges supplied men and a few came from the Plymouth exchange. It is suspected that Andersons actually used many of their own men rather than the inexperienced men originally intended for the work. Those of the unemployed who were used were not fit for the work and often unwilling to do it. Living conditions for the men were at best poor and often quite dreadful with some sleeping almost rough in the countryside. Andersons had submitted the lowest bid for the contract – £197,000 – and naturally therefore, costs were kept to the minimum wherever possible. One benefit to the local economy was that timber for the sleepers was obtained from local oak trees, which were then cut and prepared by local labour and taken the relatively short distances to where they were required. Ballast too was obtained from local quarries, as it had been

Action in the transfer shed. Shredded clay is tipped from a narrow gauge wagon to one of the standard gauge wagons for direct delivery. Manual labour is still of prime importance in the operation.
(The Ball Clay Heritage Society)

Opposite page, top: An E1/R class 0-6-2T arrives at Torrington with a train from Bideford and Barnstaple.
(Tom Bartlett Postcard Collection, Berrynarbor, EX34 9SE)

Opposite page, bottom: One of the standard-gauge ten-ton wagons that the Company hired in. Clay was loaded into these wagons at the works and taken direct to the port of embarkation.
(The Ball Clay Heritage Society)

for the Torrington & Marland over forty years earlier. The projected construction period proved hopelessly optimistic, mainly due to the exceptionally wet summers of 1923 and 1924, and work dragged on. Heavy flooding in the winter of 1924 undermined the foundations of one of the piers for the new viaduct over the Torridge. Rather than demolish and start again, the leaning pier was dragged upright and underpinned to a foundation ring blasted out of the riverbed.

Further Light Railway Orders had had to be obtained in 1922 and 1923 to increase capitalisation and extend

construction time. The work had also been interrupted by what is now know as the Hatherleigh Riot on 23rd June 1923, when a group of "drunken work-shy layabouts from Plymouth" (probably some of those referred to earlier as unwilling to work) attacked the local police sergeant. A constable and several townspeople helped him until a group of the railway navvies arrived and saw off the troublemakers, some of who later received sentences of up to 5 months hard labour. All had not gone well with the contractors either, for in February 1925 Andersons had to call in a receiver to carry

The Torrington & Marland Light Railway

on the business. This he did for a few weeks and then the redoubtable Colonel Stephens stepped in and saw the rest of the work completed. It was not therefore until 23rd July 1925 that a satisfactory Board of Trade inspection was carried out on the completed works, with the formal opening taking place on Monday, 27th July 1925.

The new line followed the course of the narrow gauge line as far as Dunsbear, where it veered away slightly to the west to avoid the Clay Company property, and then headed through Petrockstowe, Meeth, Hatherleigh, Hole, and thence to Halwill Junction where it met up with the Bude, Okehampton, and Padstow lines. Whilst these new stations, or halts, carried the names mentioned, that it not to assume that they were close to the settlements of the same name. Hatherleigh, the main station on the new line, was some two miles from the town it purported to serve and had originally been planned as Lewer Halt. In the event, the proposed station for Hatherleigh was abandoned and Lewer Halt became Hatherleigh. Hole (for Black Torrington) was so named as not to be confused with Torrington, and was actually nearer Black Torrington than Hole, and not exactly close to anywhere of size.

With the opening of the North Devon & Cornwall Junction Light Railway (NDCJLR), the Torrington & Marland Light Railway passed into history, the only 3ft gauge line remaining being the tracks in the works and clay pits area. Transfer of clay was now made to a standard gauge siding, which came off the new main line slightly further south than the old line, so as to by-pass the works and the Clay Company property. The severance of the old line just before Dunsbear, and the change in alignment of the new line, meant that the workmen had to walk from the end of the 3ft old line to the new Dunsbear Halt to catch the train home.

Whilst it was the clay of Peters Marland that would provide the main source of revenue for the new line, deposits of ball clay were present further south at Meeth. The greater distance from a port or railhead meant that these deposits were not economic to extract, and little was done until the 1920s. As we saw in Chapter 2, Eustace Holwill had retired from the North Devon Clay Company and it appears that he had moved his allegiance down the road to Meeth, for in 1920 he was appointed Managing Director of the newly formed Meeth (North Devon) Clay Company Limited. The new company did not appear to progress very quickly, for which Eustace received the blame and was forced to resign. Progress was better with a new man at the helm, but transport was a major problem with steam waggons and motor lorries causing the already inadequate roads to deteriorate. The condition of the vehicles themselves was also an increasing cause for concern. The imminent arrival of the NDCJLR was seen as the answer to their problems, and negotiations for a connection were soon concluded. The main centre of operations at Meeth was at Woolladon pit, which had been developed over the other pit at Stockleigh as it was close to the road. To transport the clay to the new railway, a 2ft gauge tramway was built, and the NDCJLR agreed to provide a transfer siding. In the event, the Meeth Company had to pay for an additional connection to the siding, thus making it a loop capable of collecting clay wagons by either up or down trains.

Although the NDCJLR provided the missing link in the railway system in the area, it was unfortunate that it did not prove to be the great success that was intended. The mistake, if such it were, was to make the link westwards between North Devon and Cornwall, rather than south to mid and south Devon via Okehampton, as had been the original idea. Such a connection would have linked Torrington and North Devon with Plymouth and Exeter and thus given a direct link

A Halwill Junction bound train near the clay works. Another E1/R passes the new access siding for the clay works with a rather short Torrington to Halwill Junction train on 15th August 1947.
(Roger Kidner)

to the main railway network. This would have provided more through freight and passenger traffic, opened up trade in North Devon to a wider market, and also disproved Sir Eric Geddes' remarks quoted earlier. The NDCJLR was in reality built more as a through tourist route than as a local service, and it was hoped by its promoters that holidaymakers would use the line on their travels along the north coasts of Devon and Cornwall. Over the years, little or no effort was made by the owning companies to improve or even publicise the route, and as it was there were no through passenger train workings, a change of train at Torrington and a wait for a connecting service was necessary (certainly not the best way to encourage traffic and increase revenue).

Although the railways were grouped into four main companies in 1923 (London Midland & Scottish, London & North Eastern, Great Western, and Southern), the NDCJLR remained an independent company until nationalisation in 1948, although it was actually worked under agreement by the Southern Railway from inception. Torrington in LSWR days had always been the main terminus of North Devon trains from Waterloo, including the "Atlantic Coast Express", and trains to Bideford and Torrington worked straight through Barnstaple Junction, taking precedence over those to Ilfracombe, which was regarded as a branch off the Torrington line. Changes were felt immediately at Torrington, as improvements were carried out at Ilfracombe, which was suddenly promoted to the main destination with Torrington relegated to a double branch terminus. There were operational difficulties on the Torrington to Halwill section in view of the lightly graded track, which prevented the heavier locomotives working south through Torrington. However, had there been the will at the right level of authority to provide a proper service, this problem could have been overcome. As John Nicholas points out in his book

Lines to Torrington, the mainstay of the motive power for the two branches were the Adams 460 class 4-4-0s and the E1/R class 0-6-2 tanks which both worked into Torrington from either end, and so could have easily worked through trains.

The Southern Railway and the Great Western Railway followed the tradition of their original constituent companies and were always fierce rivals and competitors, and the advent of British Railways in 1948 did nothing to stop this rivalry, which continued between the new Southern and Western Regions. Little happened during the first ten years or so but it was with the greatest of unease that on 1st January 1963 all lines west of Salisbury found themselves under Western Region control. This unease was well founded, for the following year saw closure proposals abounding. The official attitude towards rail services in the area was clearly highlighted shortly after this when, with effect from 7th September 1965, the Western Region withdrew freight facilities from nearly all of the stations west of Exeter. (Watergate and Dunsbear Halts had already closed from 2nd May 1960, and Torrington had lost its locomotive shed back on 2nd November 1959.)

The section from Torrington to Halwill Junction was the first to be earmarked for closure and, after a public enquiry on 2nd September 1964, closure followed on 1st March 1965 (the last day of passenger services being Saturday, 27th February) – goods services having ceased on 7th September 1964. The section from Barnstaple to Torrington was closed to passengers from 4th October 1965.

The last train to run on this part of the line was the steam hauled "Exmoor Ranger" organised by the Railway Correspondence & Travel Society on 27th March 1965. This ran from Exeter St David's to Halwill, Torrington, Barnstaple Junction, Barnstaple Victoria Road, Ilfracombe and back via Dulverton and Taunton. Two Ivatt class 2 tank locomotives

TORRINGTON.

Shunting operations.—Before a shunting movement is made from the down to the up line through No. 24 crossover road whilst a train is standing at the up platform, the Driver of such train must be advised of the intended shunting movement and instructed not to move his engine forward until the crossing movement has been completed and the line is clear.

In consequence of the severe gradient from Torrington falling in the direction of Bideford, which commences a short distance the station side of the signal box, no vehicle must be permitted to stand on the up line at any point beyond the up platform ramp at the Bideford end of Torrington station, unless an engine or brake van with a man in attendance is attached at the Bideford end of the vehicle.

J. B. Reed & Co's sidings.—Traffic for the sidings must be placed immediately beyond the gates, and traffic from the sidings accepted at the same point. Messrs. J. B. Reed & Coy. will arrange to work traffic beyond this point, and under no circumstances must the Company's engine pass inside the gates.

The portions of the sidings situated on the Railway Company's premises may be used for any traffic in connection with the railway.

Marland (North Devon Clay Co.) siding.—Upon arrival of a down train at the siding the Guard must fully apply the brake in the rear van and securely apply a sufficient number of wagon brakes to ensure that the vehicles standing on the running line remain stationary. After unlocking the siding gate and operating the ground frame, the vehicles for the siding must be drawn forward into the outer loop clear of the loop facing points. The engine must then be detached and shunted to the inner loop where it must be attached to the outgoing wagons, which will be marshalled by the Marland Clay Company's employees on that loop. The outgoing wagons must then be propelled on to that portion of the train left on the running line.

Upon arrival of an up train at the siding, ingoing wagons must be propelled by the train engine on to the outer loop and outgoing wagons drawn from the inner loop.

The Company's engine must not proceed into the siding beyond the engine restriction boards which are erected on the sidings, (1) approximately 50 yards beyond the facing connection leading from the outer loop to the Clay Company's Works, (2) approximately 25 yards beyond the trailing connection on the inner loop.

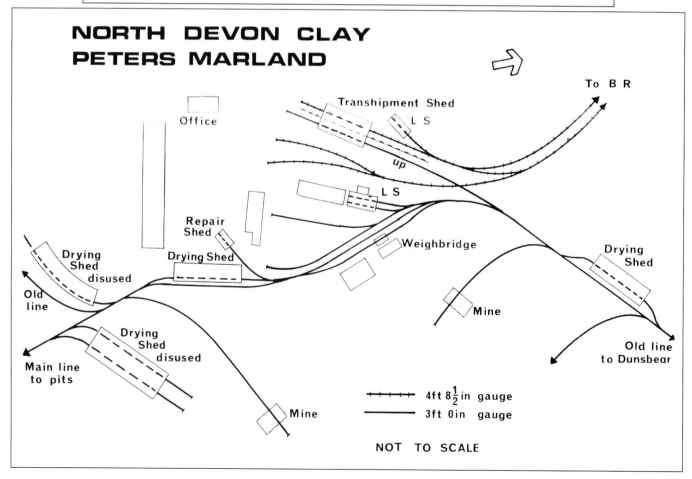

After the Narrow Gauge

Photograph of part of the Clay Works site, taken midway between the drying shed and the transhipment sheds, looking roughly south-west.
(Author's collection/John Hill) (The late Jim Peden)

Opposite page, top: Procedures for dealing with traffic from the Marland Clay Company's siding.
Extract from the Southern Railway "Appendix to Working Time Table" for 26th March 1934.

Opposite page, bottom:
Plan of the Clay Works site, showing both narrow and standard gauge lines.

numbers 41206 and 41291 were used over the NDCJLR section.

In the autumn of 1965, the section from Hatherleigh to the Meeth sidings also closed, and clay from Meeth had to travel to Torrington and onwards. Signalling on the Barnstaple – Halwill Junction line was restructured from 26th February 1967 when the number of signal boxes was reduced to three. The passing loop at Petrockstow was retained for run-round purposes. As from 20th September 1970, Torrington signal box was closed and the down road converted to a siding. (The central crossover and up sidings had been removed in 1967.) The age and condition of the dockside cranes that handled the clay at Fremington Quay led to them being withdrawn from use from 31st December 1969. Clay exports from Fremington thus ceased when the quay closed in March 1970. The following November saw the closure of the truncated remains of the 3ft gauge railway that still operated at the Marland works, and all clay was then handled by road vehicle both on and off site.

Rather strangely in retrospect, a new milk loading facility was installed at Torrington in March 1976 at the end of the main platform, although milk traffic ceased completely just over two years later on 12th October 1978. As late as April 1976 the old goods shed was rebuilt and extended for a new fertiliser depot, but this lasted only a little longer than the milk facility, closing on 11th January 1980. Clay traffic amounting to some 30,000 tons per annum was all that kept the line open after this, but the old railway wagons then used were in need of replacement. New 57 tonne railcars were to be constructed for the ECC Meeth clay, but the track was not up to the standards needed for such large vehicles. 1982 saw a strike by the rail unions ASLEF and the NUR, the former of which lasted on and off for most of the year. The road haulage industry grasped this opportunity with both hands and negotiated irresistible transport deals for traffic, which British Railways were unable at that time to carry. A few

discussions took place between British Railways and ECC (Meeth) and Watts Blake Bearne (Marland), but the whole line was closed totally from 31st August 1982, although the last trainload of clay actually travelled on 13th September.

Several strenuous attempts were made to have the line reopened for freight and passenger use, including an application for financial assistance from Europe. As part of the fact-finding mission for this, several local civic leaders, British Railways officials, local industrialists, members of the North Devon Railway Line Action Group and the Devon Member of the European Parliament, Lord O'Hagan travelled by special train – a diesel railcar – from Barnstaple to Torrington and back on 27th January 1983, but to no avail. By the end of March, the request had been turned down. The West of England Divisional Manager of British Railways promised, during the trip, that they would leave the track in situ for at least two years to allow for any further re-opening ventures. However, eighteen months later, track lifting started at the Meeth end of the line. Torrington station building stood lonely and empty until sold in October 1983, and the building reopened in March 1984 as the "Puffing Billy" pub.

Most of the old track bed from Bideford to Hatherleigh has been incorporated into the Tarka Trail, a footpath and cycleway covering approximately 180 miles of old railway and established footpaths in North and Central Devon, named after Henry Williamson's well known book about the otter of that name. A length of track remains in Torrington station, on which are currently parked a china clay wagon and a brake van. Apart from a cycle hire outlet, the old fertiliser shed and goods yard are occupied by juggernauts from a local road haulage firm. And so the railway, which was built to carry the clay and other goods, has been uprooted and destroyed. Vastly greater loads have thus been forced back on to those largely unchanged local roads, which even one hundred years ago were incapable of coping with the traffic of the area.

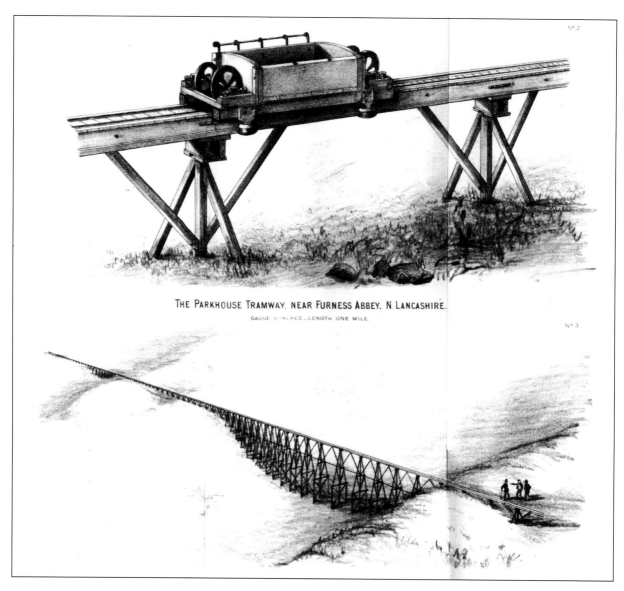

Nº 2

THE PARKHOUSE TRAMWAY, NEAR FURNESS ABBEY, N. LANCASHIRE.

GAUGE 5 INCHES...LENGTH ONE MILE.

Nº 3

THE PARKHOUSE TRAMWAY, NEAR FURNESS ABBEY, N. LANCASHIRE.

GAUGE 5 INCHES...LENGTH ONE MILE.

Chapter 7

CONCLUSIONS

John Barraclough Fell died at his home in Southport on 18th October 1902 in his 88th year. His obituary in *The Engineer* of 24th October describes him as "an engineer who possessed unusual originality, and was at one time very prominently before the world." The issue of *Engineering* of the same date carried similar words and the *Minutes of Proceedings of the Institution of Civil Engineers* was likewise complementary. He was one of the great innovative engineers of his time, but he has been somewhat under-rated and overlooked by historians; his work never seeming to receive the acclaim and recognition it deserved. Obviously held in high esteem by his peers, he was elected an Associate of the Institution of Civil Engineers on 3rd March 1883, just two years after the opening of the Torrington & Marland Railway. John B. Fell was born towards the end of the reign of George III and lived through the reigns of four more monarchs, including Queen Victoria. Being only in his mid-twenties at the time of Victoria's accession, we may class Fell as one of that small band of British Victorian engineers who did so much for the development of their country. His obituaries tell us that "although he practically retired from business many years ago, nothing gave him more pleasure than a business chat, and up to the last his mind was as vigorous and powerful as ever, and his memory, always phenomenal, never failed."

It would seem that, after the Torrington & Marland, he did gradually retire from the scene, and we have seen that his son, George Noble Fell, was taking more of a front line position with, for example, the Pentewan Railway and the negotiations concerning the North Devon & Cornwall Junction Light Railway. By 1881 John Fell's shares in the Green Odd Contracting Company had been transferred to his younger son, Frederick Offer Fell and to others. George Noble Fell was also no longer a shareholder by then. It is also interesting to note, in connection with the Green Odd Company, that one of the Fell patents – number 899 – was transferred to the Green Odd Contracting Company on 8th May 1872. No doubt this was to assist the Patent Narrow Gauge Railway Company in their marketing of the patent method of construction, by having a contractor ready and able to carry out the work for any prospective purchaser.

George Noble Fell's life was marred by personal tragedy, for on 10th November 1880, only six months after performing the ceremony of turning the first sod for the new railway on Torrington Commons, his wife Mary Elizabeth died from enteric fever and peritonitis at the early age of 25. The young couple seem to have been living in Northam, near Bideford at the time, not too far from the site of the new railway. George was however to find happiness eventually, for he met and courted the daughter of a Torrington surgeon

and local registrar of births and deaths – Sarah Honoria Hole (probably the young lady referred to in the newspaper report mentioned in Chapter 1). They were married at the parish church in Torrington on 3rd October 1888. George continued his career in railway building, following his father in becoming a respected, but not perhaps such a contentious, name in the civil engineering field. His best known, and the longest lasting of the Fell family's works, was the Snaefell Mountain Railway on the Isle of Man.

Following initial surveys in 1887-8, George envisaged a steam hauled line with Fell centre rail. However electricity was adopted as the power source and the line was built with a Fell centre rail for guidance and braking. It was opened in 1895, and survives to this day. Overseas, George carried out a survey for the proposed line to link Naples with the funicular railway up Mount Vesuvius. This was to be equipped with the Abt rack system, but in the event an alternative was built to a different route with the cheaper Strub rack system and George was not involved. In around 1910, a Fell type railway was proposed for the Furka – Oberalp Railway in Switzerland, but again this was built without Fell's involvement and on the Abt rack system. As we saw earlier, George was consulted by the Torrington & Marland Company on occasion in its early years and was a go-between with his father with advice when the Torrington – Okehampton line was under serious discussion.

John Barraclough Fell was an exceptional engineer. The areas where he either worked himself, or his designs were used, covered a large part of the world; from Furness to Cornwall and Devon; from Italy and Brazil to New Zealand, and he worked alongside some of the best engineers and contractors in the world at the time. He was without doubt fixated with the idea of his patented system for timber trestles to avoid expensive earthworks, and for long locomotives with light axle loads. This is not to denigrate his ideas, for Fell was not the only engineer to make extensive use of timber for the construction of bridges and viaducts in the building of new railways. Isambard Kingdom Brunel, the great engineer of the Great Western Railway, also made extensive use of timber especially in Devon and Cornwall, where his timber viaducts were a feature of the landscape for many years, until they were gradually replaced by structures of stone and steel. Claims that the replacement of all Brunel's timber viaducts by 1934 showed that his policy of using timber was flawed ignore the conditions prevailing at the time of their design and construction. As we have seen, timber was cheap and of very high quality and, with a design that proved itself in terms of strength and reliability over the years, Brunel's viaducts made possible the construction of the railway in the West Country within the financial constraints operating at the time. Only the failure of the supply of the raw timber, chiefly after the First World War, precluded its continued use in such structures and necessitated the replacement of the existing structures. The only readily available alternative source was Oregon pine, which had a life expectancy of only 8 years.

Replacement of timber viaducts when lines were doubled for example, was not carried out because of faults in the basic design and construction, but because the engineers of the day had other materials better suited – and priced – to their needs. It may well be argued that, had timber of the quality used by Brunel been available continually since construction, some of the smaller viaducts he built may still have been in use today. Fell's work should therefore be seen in the context of what he was trying to achieve, and in that which his contemporaries were working. It is interesting in the context of his work and patents to see the extensive use someone like Brunel was making of timber in a similar railway context. The replacements of Brunel's timber bridges with stronger and more durable materials were only taking place at the time of the Torrington & Marland's demise.

The ultra-narrow gauge Parkhouse Mineral railway must have been a good proving ground for the Fell trestle system and whilst the Pentewan railway was no doubt a useful contract, it did little to extend or illustrate his patent ideas, other than to provide a stage for his locomotive designs. Pentewan already had a perfectly sound track bed, so there was no need for viaducts, trestles or raised track. The unloading trestle at Pentewan harbour was a slight nod in this direction, but of no great importance in the scheme of things. Because the track would be laid on solid ground and not elevated in any way, and to the relatively wide gauge of 2ft 6in, there was also no need for guide wheels. The removal of the guide wheels as used with "Ariel" on the 1ft 6in gauge Aldershot military railway a few years earlier indicates that Fell was turning away from this feature as an area for development. It is most likely that he had decided that additional wheels for guidance were not really necessary, as his design of low boilered locomotives with a long wheelbase gave a low centre of gravity and good stability. However,

both he and his son George clearly felt that these additional, horizontally positioned wheels did have a use for extra traction and/or braking on difficult and mountainous routes such as Rimutaka and Snaefell. However, it is probable that Fell's initial thoughts on the Pentewan were that he could develop both the guide wheel and the trestle ideas, but once into the "nitty gritty" he would have realised that neither was to be exploited on this occasion – unless in future extensions. Such extensions to the railway were planned – George Fell was indeed offering his services in this respect in February 1879 (just about the time he and his father would be starting their work on the T&M surveys) – and these could well have incorporated Fell's elevated trestles. Whether guide wheels would have been needed or used is however very doubtful.

The Torrington & Marland Light Railway, as a part of the overall development of Fell's ideas, must be rated as a great success in that it fulfilled the purpose for which it was intended. Its Achilles' heel was, as it was always going to be, the timber bridges and viaducts. No doubt with better and more thorough maintenance, and perhaps with some iron or steel replacement of key parts, these would have lasted much longer. But it is still to the great credit of John Fell that the line lasted for virtually 45 years carrying its daily traffic come rain or shine, winter and summer, without any other apparent problem than the maintenance of the timber. It should also be borne in mind that this was not a publicly owned line with shareholders and capital behind it, but purely an extension of a relatively small local mining and manufacturing company, no doubt with little spare capital for investment. In reality, the T&M should have been built to standard gauge to save what would now be the costly transfer of clay from wagon to wagon at Torrington and to have provided a through link to Okehampton as originally envisaged. But in the prevailing circumstances of the day, it was probably a better railway than might have been expected because of the foresight of Frederick Holwill and the Clay Company in employing John Barraclough Fell to engineer and build the line on their behalf.

PATENT NARROW GUAGE RAILWAY LOCOMOTIVE LINE.—GAUGE 18 INCHES.

APPENDIXES

Appendix A. List of guests

List of guests at the cutting of the first sod ceremony, and on the inaugural run, as given in the newspaper reports of the time, with author's comments and corrections

List of guests at the ceremony for the cutting of the first sod on 26th May 1880

Mr J.B. Fell
Mr and Mrs G.N. Fell
Mr F. Holwill - The Marland Brick & Clay Works
Mr Morris, of the contractors – *perhaps from Head Office*
Mr Dolby of the LSWR – *the Torrington Stationmaster*
Mr Loveband of Fowler, Fox Brothers, bankers
Mr R.P. Hirst, the contractor's local agent
Probably also the landowners, Lord Clinton, Hon Mark Rolle, J.C. Moore-Stevens Esq, and J.G. Johnson Esq

List of guests on the inaugural run on 5th February 1881

In the first truck:

Mayor of Torrington – J.S. Farleigh Esq
Mayor of Barnstaple – W. Avery Esq
Captain Molesworth of Westward Ho! (who was instrumental in the formation of the Bideford, Westward Ho! And Appledore
Railway, of which he became a director)
R.H. Lipscomb (steward to the Hon Mark Rolle)
A.E.Y. Morley Esq (sub-agent)
G. Doe Esq (Town Clerk of Torrington)
Mr Hirst (representative of the Leeds firm of contractors) *(This is R.P. Hirst, the local agent of Green Odd Contractors)*

In the second truck:

Mr Fell, junior (J.B. Fell's son, George Noble Fell)
The representatives of the press

In the third truck:

Colonel White-Thompson of Hatherleigh
Mr Hooper of Hatherleigh
Mr F. Holwill
"and a few others"; probably including, Mr N. Chapple of Torrington, Mr H.L. Mallett,
Mr. Losetand (probably Loveband, the Manager of Fowler, Fox Brothers, the Clay Company's Bankers),
Mr T. Fowler, Mr Dalby (Mr Dolby, the LSWR stationmaster at Torrington), and Mr Ruhe.

On the locomotive:
Mr J.B. Fell

Appendix B. 3 foot gauge steam locomotives: 1879 – 1925

"Mary" (number 1, works number 576). Built by Black Hawthorn in 1880, in use from 1880 to 1925.				
Wheel arrangement	**Diameter of wheels**	**Wheelbase**	**Cylinders**	**Boiler**
0-6-0 ST	1ft 8in	9 feet	7.5in x 10in	120psi

"Tudor/Kent" (works number 265). Built by W G Bagnall in 1879, hired in for 18 months from 7th March 1883.				
Wheel arrangement	**Diameter of wheels**	**Cylinders**	**Firebox**	**Tubes**
0-4-0 inverted ST	1ft 6in	6in x 9in (inside cylinders)	Copper	Brass

"Marland" (number 2, works number 566). Built by W G Bagnall in 1883, in use from 1883 to 1925.					
Wheel arrangement	**Diameter of wheels**	**Wheelbase**	**Cylinders**	**Firebox**	**Tubes**
0-6-0 T	1ft 8in	9ft	7.5in x 10in	Copper	Brass

"Peter" (number 3). Built by Stephen Lewin circa 1871, in use from circa 1884, gone by 1923.			
Wheel arrangement	**Diameter of wheels**	**Wheelbase**	**Cylinders**
0-4-0 T	1ft 9in	9ft	5.75in x 9in

"Coffeepot"? Built by Head Wrightson? Scrapped circa 1908.	
Wheel arrangement	**Boiler**
0-4-0 T	Vertical

"Avonside" (number 11, works number 1428). Built by Avonside in 1901, in use from 1901 to circa 1925.			
Wheel arrangement	**Diameter of wheels**	**Wheelbase**	**Cylinders**
0-6-0 ST	1ft 8in	9ft	7in x 10in

"Jersey I" (works number 129). Built by Fletcher Jennings in 1873, in use from August 1908 to 1949. Scrapped October 1949.				
Wheel arrangement	**Diameter of wheels**	**Cylinders**	**Boiler**	**Tubes**
0-4-0 ST (later converted to tender engine)	2ft 9in	9in x 16in	7ft 3.5in x 2ft 9in. 78 1.5in diameter tubes.	Brass

"Jersey II" (works number 139). Built by Fletcher Jennings in 1874, in use from August 1908 to 1949. Scrapped March 1952.				
Wheel arrangement	**Diameter of wheels**	**Cylinders**	**Boiler**	**Tubes**
0-4-0 ST (later converted to tender engine)	2ft 9in	9in x 16in	7ft 3.5in x 2ft 9in. 78 1.5in diameter tubes.	Brass

"Merton" (also known as "Jersey III") (works number 150). Built by Fletcher Jennings in 1875, in use from August 1908 to 1949. Scrapped October 1949.				
Wheel arrangement	**Diameter of wheels**	**Cylinders**	**Boiler**	**Tubes**
0-4-0 ST	2ft 9in	9in x 16in	7ft 3.5in x 2ft 9in. 78 1.5in diameter tubes.	Brass

Appendix C. Bill of quantities

Earthworks:				
Light bank and cutting up to 3 feet in depth	8,500 cubic yards			
Bank and cutting exceeding 3 feet in depth	21,000 cubic yards	29,500 cubic yards		
Masonry		150 cubic yards		
Permanent way:		Tons	Cwts	Qtrs
Rails – 30lb per linear yard		295	0	0
Fish plates and bolts		25	0	0
Dog nails and spikes		7	0	0
Fang bolts		6	5	0
Sleepers: 6ft x 8ft x 4in	8976			
Sleepers: 4ft 6in x 7ft x 3in	4224	13200		
Foot plank and guard rail in viaducts	Timber	2000 cubic feet		
Ballast		7500 cubic yards		
Viaducts:				
Timber work:		Cubic feet		
70 chains averaging 5ft in height		6.407		
49 chains averaging 10ft in height		5.703		
22 chains averaging 15ft in height		3.056		
11 chains averaging 20ft in height		1.656		
2 chains averaging 25ft in height		.461		
1 chains averaging 30ft in height		.228		
4 chains averaging 35ft in height		1.212		
Bridge over the River Torridge		2.783		
	Total:	21.566		
Iron work:		Tons	Cwts	Qtrs
Bolts		25	6	2
Plates & washers		10	8	0
Spikes		2	0	0
	Total:	37	14	2
Castings			18	0
Shoes for foundation piles			7	1
Viaducts:		M	F	Ch
Average height 5ft			7	0
Average height 10ft			4	9
Average height 15ft			2	2
Average height 20ft			1	1
Average height 25ft				2
Average height 30ft				1
Average height 35ft				4

Description				
Bridge over the River Torridge				3
Total length of viaduct		2	0	2
Cutting under 3ft in depth		1	0	8
Cutting over 3ft in depth			6	3
Bank formed out of cuttings		1	4	2
Surface line			6	5
Total length of railway		6	2	0
Stations:				
Sidings, points and crossings, level crossings, signals, engine shed, water tanks, turntable, etc, as per specification		£750. 0. 0d.		
Rolling stock:				
1 locomotive engine		£850. 0. 0d.		
20 wagons @ £45 each		£900. 0. 0d.		

Appendix D. Schedule of prices

Schedule of prices to regulate the monthly payments on account of materials and works executed.

Description of Material Works etc.	Quantity	Price
Sleepers: Oak 6ft 0in x 7in x 3 1/2in, Red Pine 6ft x 8ft x 4ft	Each	2/-
Bolts and plates for viaducts and bridges fish plate and fang bolts and dog nails	Per ton	£15
Ballast delivered along the line	Per cubic yard	2/6d
Permanent way complete (without rails) with sleepers and fastenings and ballast	Per linear yard	7/-
Baltic red pine and other timber and deals planks scaffolding etc.	Per cubic foot	2/-
Bolts washers and fish plates for viaduct work	Per ton	£17
Lattice girders complete: 15 feet long	Each	£1.13.0d.
Lattice girders complete: 18 feet long	Each	£2. 2. 0d.
Viaduct supports complete: drawing numbers 4, 5 and 5a	Per foot of height	4/-
Viaduct supports complete: drawing numbers 7 and 8	Per foot of height	6/-
Work executed in bridge over the Torridge and viaduct drawings numbers 9 and 10	Per cubic foot	3/10d.
Forming line earthworks in cuttings and embankments:		
– not exceeding 6 feet in depth	Per linear yard	5/-
– exceeding 6 feet in depth	Per cubic yard	1/4d.
Rubble masonry in bridges etc.	Per cubic yard	17/6d.
Brick work in arches	Per cubic yard	30/-